15 of 20
August 1965

The Book of the PROMISES OF GOD

Presented to Peter Berg

Sept 18, 1977

Bill Blackwell

4th

Sunday Church School

The Book of the

PROMISES
OF GOD

By Marjorie Garhart

Illustrated by Tom Irons

Gustav K. Wiencke, *Editor*

Lutheran Church Press, Philadelphia

LCA SUNDAY CHURCH SCHOOL SERIES

This pupil's Reader is accompanied by three pupil's Workbooks and by a Teacher's Guide, each titled *The Book of the Promises of God*. These materials have been prepared for use in a three-term course in the Sunday Church School (4-1,2,3).

LB 138-9865K65

CONTENTS

Part 1

Stories from Genesis

1. From the Beginning

Through all the long years since the world was very young, people have wondered: How did it all begin? And why? No one knows how many people have said, "I wonder how, and I wonder why."

At what time God began to put the answers in people's hearts, no one knows. But somewhere, sometime, in the very, very long, long ago, men began to understand that the universe was created by God, who is loving and good. They began to understand that God made them and wanted them to know and love and serve him. Without God the world would not be and they would not be.

And in that long ago time one man told a story which says the things that God had showed him. The story is written in the beginning of the very first book of the Bible. It is the story of creation.

In the beginning God created the heavens and the earth.
But the earth had no shape, and there was darkness everywhere.
And God said, "Let there be light."
And there was light.
And God saw that the light was good.
And he called the light Day, and the darkness he called Night.

Then God separated the earth from the heavens
And gathered the waters into rivers and lakes and seas.
And when the dry land appeared, God said,
"Now let plants grow and fruit trees bloom
And let their seed and their fruit be everywhere."
And God saw that it was good.

And God said, "Let there be lights in the heavens to separate
    the day from the night.
And let them mark the seasons and the days and the years."
And it was so. God made two great lights,
A greater light to rule the day and a lesser light to rule the night.
He made the stars also.
And he saw that it was good.

And God said, "Let living creatures be in the waters,
Swarms of fish and great sea monsters;
And let birds fly across the heavens."
And God saw that it was good.

From the Beginning   11

And God said, "Let there be living creatures on the earth,
Creeping things and beasts and cattle."
And it was so, and it was good.

Then God said, "I will make a special creature,
Not like the animals of the field
Not like the birds of the air
Not like the fish of the sea.
I will breathe into him my own breath
So that he can know me and love me and talk with me,
And I will let him rule for me over earth and air and sea."
So God created Man and Woman,
And he blessed them, and gave them all the gifts of his creation
To love and use and take care of.

And God saw everything that he had made,
And behold, it was very good!

WHAT WENT WRONG?

God made the whole world, and that world was good—but what went wrong? Why do people so often do things that make themselves and other people unhappy?

These are the questions another man asked himself long ago. And he also put into a story the answer which God helped him know. It is the second story in the Book of Genesis, a "book of beginnings."

STORIES FROM GENESIS

And the Lord God made a beautiful garden in Eden, filled with trees and flowers and sunlight and rich earth. Birds sang in the garden and animals played there. And God put Man and Woman into his good garden to take care of it and enjoy the fruit of many trees in it. This was a good life, beautiful and full of love. And Man and Woman were happy because they were doing the things for which God had made them.

Everything in the garden was theirs to enjoy—except one thing. "Do not touch the Tree in the center of the garden," God said, "and do not eat any of its fruit, or you will surely die."

Now the Serpent was in the garden, and the Serpent was cunning and evil. "What harm could there be in tasting such beautiful fruit?" the Serpent said to the Woman one day. "You will not really die. You will be like God, and then you will know both good and evil."

The Woman looked at the beautiful Tree. She smelled its fragrant flowers. She wanted to taste the bright fruit that hung heavy from its branches. And because she had been told not to touch it, she wanted it very much indeed! She wanted the fruit to make her as wise as God. So she did the thing God had told her not to do. She picked the fruit and ate it and gave some to her husband to eat.

As soon as Man and Woman had eaten it, they knew that they had done something very wrong. They had disobeyed God. God had made them and trusted them, and they had broken his rule for them. They were ashamed. It was wrong to think they could be just like God. And they were afraid. Now they knew they did not deserve God's love. So they hid in the bushes and hoped God would not find them.

But when God called, the Man and the Woman knew God would always find them. And God said, "Have you eaten of the Tree which I told you not to touch?"

"It was the Woman's fault," said the Man. "She picked the fruit and gave it to me to eat."

"It was the Serpent's fault," said the Woman. "The Serpent tricked me into eating the fruit."

But God said, "Both of you have disobeyed me, and so you may not have the happy life I planned for you." Sadly, God sent Man and Woman out of the beautiful garden of Eden. An angel with a flaming sword stood guard so that they could never return.

THE BIBLE'S STORY

The story of Adam and Eve is really the story of every person who has ever lived. Every person spoils God's good plan for him by choosing the things *he* wants to do instead of the things *God* wants him to do.

How can we ever get back the happy life with God that he wants for us and that we spoil by disobeying him? We could never do it by ourselves. But the Bible tells the long story of what God did and still does to win his people back and make them belong to him again.

2. *Abraham and God's Promise*

Long, long ago, nearly two thousand years before Jesus was born, in a time when men did not know the God who made them and prayed instead to the stars and the moon and thought that the sun was a god—in those far-off times there lived a wandering shepherd chief named Abram.

The tents of Abram and his tribe spread like a family of black shadows in a grassy land called the Plain of Aram. Nearby was the city of Haran. From its gate a highway stretched over the horizon to faraway Babylonia. This grassy plain had been Abram's home for many years. Here Abram had become head of the tribe when his father died. Here Abram cared for his large flocks of sheep and goats. Abram knew and loved this land, and his life here was quiet and good. If he was sad at all, it was because he and his wife Sarai were growing old and they had no children.

And then one day something happened to change Abram's whole life—and ours, too, as you will see. God spoke to Abram.

GOD SPEAKS TO ABRAM

Abram did not know the one God who made the world. People then believed in many gods. But God said to Abram:

"Go from your country and your people and your father's house to the land that I will show you. And I will make of you a great nation, and I will bless you, and make your name great, so that you will be a blessing. . . . And because of you all the families of the earth will bless themselves."

So Abram went, as God had told him. With him went his wife Sarai, his nephew Lot and all of Lot's family, and the servants and shepherds and their families. They rolled up the

STORIES FROM GENESIS

black goat-hair tents and their blankets and clothes. They gathered their weapons and tools. They filled sacks with grain and goatskin bags with water. They loaded the donkeys with all they could carry and gathered the sheep and goats. And they all went with Abram away from the home they loved on the Plain of Aram.

They traveled south and west for many days. Then they crossed the Jordan River and came into the land of Canaan. Other people were living in Canaan, but there was room for Abram with all of his tribe and all of his animals. Abram looked for grass in the hills and wells in the valleys for watering his flocks. He looked for safe places to pitch the black tents. Slowly he took his flocks from one grassy place to another through the strange country until he came to a place called

Shechem. And while Abram and his tribe were camped there, God came again to Abram and said: "To your descendants I will give this land."

Abram believed God. He took stones and built an altar. He thanked God for bringing him safely into the land as he had promised. Wherever Abram camped he built an altar and burned on it an offering of thanks to God. And each altar stood to remind people that Abram trusted a God who made promises and would keep them.

Years went by. Abram did not forget God, who had called him to come to this new land and had promised to give the land to his children and his children's children. But still Abram did not have a son.

And God spoke to Abram again and gave him a great hope. "Lift up your eyes, and look . . . northward and south-ward and eastward and westward; for all the land which you see I will give to you and to your descendants for ever."

In wonderful ways God spoke to Abram and promised to give him as many grandchildren and great, great grandchildren as the stars of the sky or grains of dust on the earth.

And Abram believed God.

GOD MAKES A COVENANT WITH ABRAHAM

Sometimes in the night, when Abram looked up at the stars overhead, he wondered, "How could God ever do what he has promised? I am very old," Abram thought, "and my wife is old; we are too old to have children. And without

STORIES FROM GENESIS

children, how can I be the father of a great nation that will someday bring happiness to the whole world?" But even though he did not understand how it could ever be, Abram trusted that God would keep his promise. And God was pleased because Abram believed him.

So God said to Abram, "Trust me always, and you shall be the father of many nations." And God changed Abram's name to Abraham because he would become a father of many nations. He gave Sarai the name Sarah, which means "princess."

And God said, "I will be your God and your children's God forever." So God came close to Abraham and his family in a very special way, and the promises they made to each other are called a covenant.

WHEN GOD TESTED ABRAHAM

Sarah was old when her son was born. How she had once laughed to think that she, an old woman, would have a child! Abraham and Sarah named the baby *Isaac,* which means "laughter." They gave him this name to tell of the surprise and joy he brought to them. Abraham and Sarah loved Isaac more than anything else in the world, and they thanked God for this great gift.

When Isaac was young, his family moved to Beersheba. Here God told Abraham to do a strange and frightening thing: "Take your son Isaac, whom you love, and go to a mountain in the land of Moriah," God told Abraham. "And when you get there, you must offer him as a burnt offering."

So Abraham got up early in the morning, saddled his donkey, and took two servants and his son Isaac with him. He cut wood for the burnt offering, and then went to the place God had told him. When they got there, Abraham said to his servants, "Stay here with the donkey. The boy and I will go up the mountain to worship alone."

So Isaac carried the wood for the offering, and Abraham carried the knife and a pot of coals for the fire. They went up together to the place of offering.

And Isaac said to Abraham, "My father!"

And Abraham answered, "I am here, my son."

"My father," Isaac said, "I see the fire and the wood, but where is the lamb for a burnt offering?"

And Abraham said gently, "God will provide his own lamb, my son."

When they came to the place God had told him about, Abraham built an altar and laid the wood on the altar. He lifted his son onto the altar. Then he drew out his knife.

But at that very moment God called to him, "Abraham, Abraham!"

Abraham said, "Here I am."

And God said, "Do not hurt the child. For now I know that you love God even more than you love your son."

Abraham looked up and saw a ram. It was caught in a thicket. Abraham took the ram and offered it instead of his son. And the name of that place was called forever after, "The LORD will provide."

3. Caretakers of God's Promise

When Isaac became a man, he married Rebekah, a beautiful woman who lived not far from the city of Haran. And God promised Isaac, as he had promised Abraham: "I will be with you and bless you. I will give this land to you and to your children and your children's children, and they will bring my blessing to all the nations of the earth." And Isaac believed God, just as his father Abraham had believed.

Isaac had twin sons, Jacob and Esau. But even though they were twins, Jacob and Esau were not alike at all! Esau's strong arms were covered with red hair, but Jacob's arms were smooth. Esau loved to be outdoors and go hunting; Jacob liked to stay in the tent. Esau had been born first. He knew that some day his father would bless him and give him the right to be head of the tribe. But Jacob was jealous of Esau. He wanted to be head of the tribe himself. So Jacob looked for a way to trick Esau out of his father's blessing.

One day Jacob saw his chance. Isaac was very old and nearly blind. He thought that he could not live much longer. So the old father asked Esau to hunt for a gazelle and cook it the way he liked it. "When I have eaten," Isaac said, "I will give you my blessing."

Jacob heard what his old father told Esau. As soon as Esau was gone, Jacob dressed in Esau's clothes. He covered his hands and the smooth part of his neck with hairy goatskins. Then he took his father a dinner of tender goat meat which his mother had made to taste like gazelle meat.

"I have brought the food, my father," Jacob said.

The voice sounded to the old father like Jacob's voice, so he asked, "Who are you?"

Jacob answered, "I am Esau."

"Come near," Isaac said, "so that I may touch you."

Jacob held out his hand to his blind father, and Isaac felt the hairy skin. "The voice is Jacob's voice," Isaac thought, "but the hands are the hands of Esau."

So Isaac gave his blessing to Jacob, thinking he was Esau. And because in those days a blessing could never be taken back after it had been spoken, Jacob now had the right to be chief when Isaac died.

When Esau found out, he hated Jacob. "I will kill my brother Jacob," he said.

Jacob was afraid to stay at home. He ran away from home and started toward Haran, where his Uncle Laban lived.

The way to Haran was long, and when ni̤ Jacob slept under the stars. And he dreamed of a ladder th. reached up and up to heaven. In the dream he saw angels moving up and down the ladder! Above stood God saying:

"I am the LORD, the God of Abraham your father and the God of Isaac; the land on which you lie I will give to you and to your descendants; and your descendants . . . shall spread abroad to the west and to the east and to the north and to the south; and by you and your descendants shall all the families of the earth bless themselves. Behold, I am with you and will keep you wherever you go, and will bring you back here."

Then Jacob woke up. He was afraid. "Surely the Lord is in this place, and I did not know it," he said.

When morning came, Jacob took the stone which had been his pillow and set it up to mark the place. And he called the place Bethel, which means "the house of God." God had made the same covenant with Jacob. Now it was Jacob's turn to be the caretaker of God's promise.

Many years later, Jacob and his family returned to the land of Canaan. Jacob was now very rich, and he had a large family. Other things were different about Jacob, too. God had changed him from a person who would cheat his brother into a person who could be the leader of God's special people. Even Jacob's name was changed. His new name was Israel. Someday his descendants would also be called "Israel." But before that happened, Jacob and his family had to leave Canaan.

4. Joseph and His Brothers

Jacob wept. Of all his twelve sons, he had loved young Joseph the best. But now he held in his hands the robe with the long sleeves which he had made for Joseph. The beautiful robe was stained with blood. Jacob wept for his lost boy. Joseph must be dead—killed by some wild beast. His brothers said they had found the robe and had brought it home to show Jacob.

Jacob did not know that his sons were lying to him. Joseph was not dead. His brothers had sold him to slave traders for twenty pieces of silver. Then the brothers had killed a goat and dipped Joseph's robe into the goat's blood. They had made up a story to tell their father.

Joseph's brothers were jealous because their father loved Joseph much more than he loved them. And they hated the boy Joseph because he had often bragged that he was better than they! Once he had told them about his dream. Joseph had dreamed that he and his brothers were tying stalks of wheat into bundles. Suddenly Joseph's bundle stood straight up and his brother's bundles bowed down to it, just the way people bow to a king! "Someday you will all bow down to me," Joseph had boasted. That had made his brothers hate him more than ever.

Now the brothers were sure they had gotten rid of Joseph for good. "We'll never see that dreamer again," they whispered.

But they were wrong.

JOURNEY TO EGYPT

Joseph was frightened. Nights on the desert were bitter cold. Strong winds whipped stinging bits of sand against his skin and into his eyes. Somewhere jackals howled. Every night Joseph knew the slave traders had taken him farther and farther away from home. He did not know where they were taking him or what would happen to him.

One day the caravan crossed into Egypt. This was rich green country, full of palm trees and beautiful plants and flowers. Soon the gates of the pharaoh's city, Avaris, opened like welcoming arms to the traders. Joseph stared in amazement at the paved streets and the great, white stone buildings that shone like gold in the warm sun. Never had the shepherd boy seen such a city! Everywhere he saw strange things. He saw a picture of a man with the head of a hawk. He saw a statue with the head of a cow. These were Egypt's gods. The people of Egypt knew nothing about Joseph's God, the God of Abraham and Isaac and Jacob. They worshiped Horus, the hawk-headed god of the sun and creator of the world. The Egyptians thought the pharaoh was a god, too.

Merchants and visitors from many nations filled the marketplace. The slave traders grinned. This was a good place to sell the boy. They knew he was no ordinary slave. Joseph was intelligent and strong and had good manners. Such a boy should bring a very good price!

IN THE HOUSE OF POTIPHAR

Potiphar, the captain of the pharaoh's guard, bought Joseph. And God was with Joseph and helped him to be a good servant. Potiphar was so pleased with Joseph that he put him in charge of all his business. He became the trusted manager of Potiphar's great house and fields.

For a long time everything went well. Then trouble came. Potiphar's wife loved the good-looking slave. She wanted Joseph to love her, too. But Joseph knew it would be wrong to steal his master's wife.

"My master trusts me," he said to her. "How can I do this great wickedness against him and against God?"

Then Potiphar's wife became very angry. She told her husband that Joseph loved her and had tried to steal her from him. Potiphar believed the lie and put Joseph into prison.

STORIES FROM GENESIS

DREAMS

Wherever Joseph went the Lord was with him—even in prison. The keeper of the prison made Joseph his assistant. When two of the prisoners had dreams they could not understand, Joseph told them what the dreams meant. And the dreams came true!

Two long years went by. And then one night the pharaoh had a dream. He dreamed that he was standing on the bank of the River Nile. Suddenly seven fat cows came out of the water and began to eat the reeds along the river. Then seven more cows, starved and thin, came out of the water and ate the seven fat cows! When the pharaoh woke up, he was troubled. He did not know what his dream meant, but he was sure it meant something. He sent for his wise men, but nobody could tell what his dream meant.

Then someone remembered that Joseph had told the prisoners the meaning of their dreams. So the pharaoh ordered Joseph to be brought to him.

Joseph listened carefully while the pharaoh told his dream. Then he said, "God is showing you what will happen. The seven fat cows stand for seven years when there will be much food and good crops. The seven starved cows stand for seven dry years when there will be no rain and no food. Now let Pharaoh choose a wise and good man to be a governor over Egypt. During the seven good years, let him store away some of the grain. Then during the seven dry years this food will save us, and the people of the land will not die."

"Because your God has showed you all this," the pharaoh said, "there is no one wiser than you. You shall be in charge. You shall be governor. And all my people will do as you command. No one except me will have more power."

From prison to palace in one day! Joseph, the favorite son of Jacob, was now the favorite of the pharaoh.

Everything happened just as Joseph had said. For seven years the harvests were rich. Joseph had great storehouses built to hold the grain. He saved up so much grain that no one could measure it.

Then the seven dry years began. In Egypt and in all the lands around, there was no rain and there was no food. So Joseph opened the storehouses and sold grain to the Egyptians. Soon people from other lands began to come to the pharaoh to buy grain to save their families from starvation.

Jacob also heard that there was grain in Egypt. And he said to his sons, "Go down and buy grain so that we may not starve to death."

So ten of the sons of Jacob went down to Egypt to buy grain, but Benjamin, Jacob's youngest son, stayed behind with his father.

Everyone who came to Egypt had to ask Joseph for permission to buy grain because Joseph was the governor. So the ten sons of Jacob came to the brother whom they had sold many years before. But they did not recognize Joseph. In his beautiful robes he looked like a prince. On his finger he wore the signet ring of the pharaoh and around his neck hung a chain of pure gold.

The ten brothers bowed low before the governor. Joseph knew them immediately and remembered how he had once dreamed that his brothers' bundles of grain bowed to his bundle.

But Joseph pretended that he did not recognize them. He spoke roughly. "Where are you from?"

"We are from Canaan. We have come to buy food."

"You are spies!" Joseph said.

Then the brothers were frightened. "No, my lord, we have come to buy food! We are honest men. We are not spies."

"You are lying," Joseph said. "You have come to spy on us."

Now the brothers were even more frightened and puzzled. They tried to explain. "We are not spies. We are a family of brothers from the land of Canaan. Once there were twelve of us, but one of our brothers is dead and one is with our father."

"I do not believe you," Joseph said. And he put them all in prison for three days.

On the third day Joseph called them to him. "I will give you a chance to prove yourselves. One of you must stay here in prison. The rest of you—go, carry grain to your families. Then bring your youngest brother here to me."

Now the brothers began to think about the wrong they had done when they had sold their brother Joseph into slavery. "Surely God is punishing us now for our sin," they decided.

So one brother, Simeon, stayed in prison while the others loaded sacks of grain to take home. On the way home, when the brothers stopped to feed their donkeys, each found in his sack the money he had paid for his grain!

Now they trembled with fear! "What is this that God has done to us?" they asked each other. The governor had thought they were spies; now he might think they were stealing!

BENJAMIN

When the brothers came home, they told their old father all that had happened. "I have already lost two sons," said Jacob. "Joseph is dead and Simeon is in prison. I cannot lose Benjamin, too." Jacob refused even to think about sending Benjamin to Egypt.

But when all the grain was gone, Jacob decided that his sons would have to go back to Egypt to buy more grain. And so he allowed Benjamin to go with them.

"I will take care of him," Judah promised his father. "I promise I will bring him back."

Then Jacob said, "If it must be so, then take gifts of the best fruits we have. And take back the money you found in your sacks."

And Jacob watched sadly as his sons set out for Egypt.

When Joseph saw that Benjamin was with his brothers, he invited them to his house for dinner. He brought Simeon out of prison, and he refused to take back the money his brothers tried to return to him. "It is not mine," he said. "I received your money. Your God must have put treasure in your sacks." Joseph did not tell them who he was or that he had put the money back in their sacks.

"Is your father well?" Joseph asked.

"He is well," they answered, and they bowed down to him.

Then Joseph saw Benjamin and asked, "Is this your younger brother? God be gracious to you, my son!"

And because he loved him so much, he went away into his own room where he could be alone. There he wept because he loved Benjamin so.

When it was time for the brothers to leave, Joseph gave secret instructions to his steward. "Fill the men's sacks with as much grain as they can carry. Put each man's money back in

his sack, and put my silver cup in the sack of the youngest brother."

Early in the morning, the brothers started home. They had not gone far when Joseph's steward caught up with them and stopped them.

"My master has sent me after you," he said. "Why have you returned evil for good? Why have you stolen his silver cup?"

"Stolen his cup!" the brothers said. "What are you talking about? We would not steal his cup! We even brought back the money we found in our sacks before. Here, search our packs. If any of us has the cup, we will all be your slaves."

Joseph's steward searched each sack, beginning with the oldest brother and ending with the youngest. And the silver cup was found in Benjamin's sack!

Then the brothers returned to the city and bowed low before Joseph. And Joseph said to them, "What is this terrible thing you have done?"

Judah replied, "What can we say? How can we clear ourselves? We shall all be your slaves."

But Joseph said, "That would not be fair. Only the man in whose sack the cup was found will be my slave. The rest of you may go in peace to your father's house."

Then Judah stepped forward and said, "Please, my lord, listen to me. Our father is old. His youngest son is very dear to him. Years ago his favorite son died; if we should go home now without this son whom he loves, then he will die, too. I could not do that! Let me stay and be your slave, and let Benjamin go back with his brothers."

Then Joseph could not keep his secret any longer. Tears streamed down his face. He said, "I am Joseph. I am your brother."

His brothers were amazed and could not answer him. They trembled. What would happen to them? What would Joseph do to punish them now?

"Don't be afraid," Joseph said. "You meant evil, but God meant it for good. He sent me here so that I would be able to save his people. He has been with me and has made me ruler over Egypt. Now hurry, go to my father and tell him that I want him to come here to live, for the famine will last five more years. Tell him how rich Egypt is and bring him here."

So Joseph's brothers returned home with their glad news.

And God came to Jacob in a dream and said, "Do not be afraid to go to Egypt; for there I will make you a great nation. I will be with you in Egypt, and some day I will bring your people back to the land of Canaan."

So Jacob and his large family went to live in Egypt, and the pharaoh let them settle in Goshen, where there was grass for their sheep and their herds of cattle.

When Jacob died, Joseph buried him in the land of Canaan where Abraham and Isaac were buried. And Joseph became the head of the family of Israel.

THE FORGOTTEN COVENANT

Years went by. The famine was over, but the sons of Jacob did not go back to Canaan. Their sons and grandsons stayed in Egypt, too. Long after Joseph and his brothers were dead, the growing family of Hebrews stayed in a land that was not their home.

New pharaohs ruled Egypt. They did not remember Joseph and did not care that he had once saved the nation from famine. The new rulers did not like the strange Hebrew farmers and shepherds who lived in a green and rich part of Egypt.

They were afraid, too, because each year there were many more Hebrews. The Egyptians did not like the way the Hebrews kept to themselves, either. Perhaps the Hebrews would someday rule the whole country!

STORIES FROM GENESIS

Then came a pharaoh who made the Hebrews his slaves and put them to work for him. Now the Hebrews had to make bricks and mortar and carry heavy stone to build two new cities, Pithom and Raamses. Taskmasters stood over them with leather whips while they worked—dragging, pulling, pushing, stamping.

It was harder now for the Hebrews to believe that God had once made a covenant with them. The stories about a land which God had promised to Abraham and Isaac and Jacob long ago did not seem true anymore. The Hebrews wanted to believe that God had promised to be with them and make them a great nation that would bring blessing to all the world. But most of the time they felt frightened and alone and very far away from God. Only a few Hebrews remembered to worship the God who had made the covenant with their fathers.

How could God's promises ever come true now?

Part 2

In the Time of Moses

NO OTHER GODS
A HOLY NAME
A HOLY DAY
HONOR PARENTS

5. Moses and God's Great Rescue

At the foot of a great rocky height called the Mountain of God, in a silent and treeless land, a shepherd named Moses was tending sheep. This was a strange place for a man to be who had grown up in an Egyptian palace. How Moses, a Hebrew, grew up in a palace and how he became a desert shepherd is a long story.

Before Moses was born, the pharaoh had made a law: every Hebrew baby boy must be drowned in the River Nile! But Moses' mother hid her baby in a basket in the reeds along the river. She chose a place where the pharaoh's daughter often came to bathe. And there the princess found the baby and took him home to be her son.

So Moses grew up in the palace of the pharaoh. He was given an Egyptian name and was brought up as a prince. Yet Moses could never forget that his own people were the pharaoh's slaves. It hurt him to see them working as slaves. Under the blistering sun they mixed wet mud and straw to make bricks for the new cities the pharaoh was building. At night Moses could hear Hebrew mothers sing sad lullabies to their children.

Many times Moses wondered about the stories he had heard—how God had spoken to Abraham and to Isaac and to Jacob, how he had promised to make the descendants of Abraham a great nation and a blessing to all the world.

One day Moses saw an Egyptian beating a Hebrew slave. Moses became very angry. He struck the Egyptian so hard that the man fell down dead. Moses buried his body in the sand. But someone told the pharaoh what Moses had done. So Moses ran away from Egypt and went to a desert land called Midian. There he married a daughter of a desert chief and helped to take care of his father-in-law's sheep.

THE BURNING BUSH

On a day that began like any other day, Moses walked along the desert ridge he knew so well. He knew where he could find patches of grass for the sheep. He had been here many times before. Each bush and plant, every pile of rocks had been like a friend to him in many lonely days and nights.

Suddenly Moses stopped and stared. A desert bush was blazing with colors that glowed like flames—red and orange, flickering wisps of pale blue-violet. The bush was on fire! But even though it was burning, it did not turn to ashes.

Moses and God's Great Rescue

"How can this be?" Moses wondered, and moved closer.

Then Moses stopped in fear. He heard a voice in the stillness of the desert. It came from the blazing bush.

"Moses, Moses!"

And Moses answered, "Here am I."

"Do not come near," the voice continued. "Take off your shoes, for the place where you are standing is holy ground. I am the God of your father, the God of Abraham, the God of Isaac, and the God of Jacob."

And Moses hid his face, for he was afraid to look at God.

Then God said, "I have seen the trouble of my people in Egypt, and I have heard their cry. I have come to save them from the Egyptians and to bring them to a good land, a land flowing with milk and honey."

"Save my people! But *how?*" Moses wondered. How could God make the pharaoh let his slaves go?

"I will send you to Pharaoh," God continued, "so that you may bring my people out of Egypt."

Moses was astonished. How could he dare go back to the land from which he had escaped?

"Who am I that I should go to Pharaoh?" he asked, trembling.

God answered, "I will be with you. And when you have brought the people out of Egypt, you shall serve me on this mountain."

"What if they ask me who you are?" Moses objected. "What can I say?"

IN THE TIME OF MOSES

"Say this," God told him. "The Lord, the God of your fathers, the God of Abraham, of Isaac, and of Jacob has sent me to you. He promises he will bring you out of your trouble in Egypt and lead you to the good land of Canaan."

"But they won't believe me!" Moses said. "They will say it isn't true!"

Then God told Moses to throw down his shepherd's rod. When he did, it turned into a snake! Moses backed away from it in fright. But God said, "Pick it up by the tail." When Moses did, it became a rod again.

"Now put your hand inside your robe," God said. Moses did, and when he took it out, it was covered with white sores. But when God told him to put it back into his robe, it was healed again.

"If they will not believe you," God said, "I will do wondrous deeds to prove that you have come to speak for me."

"But I am not a good speaker," Moses said. "I do not speak well at all."

"Who made man's mouth?" God said. "Who makes a man see and hear and speak? Is it not I, the Lord? Then go, and I will be with you and teach you what to say."

"Oh, God," Moses prayed, "please, send someone else."

Then the Lord was angry. "I will send your brother Aaron with you, and he will speak to the people for you. I have chosen you. You will tell Aaron what I want him to say. You will go to Pharaoh! You will lead my people out of Egypt!"

Moses and Aaron gathered together all the chief men of the people of Israel and told them of God's plan and promises. And when the people heard that God cared about them and their suffering and was going to save them, they bowed their heads and worshiped.

But the pharaoh would not listen to Moses and Aaron.

"Who is 'the Lord' that I should listen to him and let Israel go?" the pharaoh said angrily. "I do not know 'the Lord,' and I will not let Israel go. Why do you take the people away from their work? Get back to your burdens."

The pharaoh made up his mind to punish the Hebrews for listening to Moses and Aaron. So he told the taskmasters and the foremen of the people of Israel: "Do not give the people any more straw to make bricks; from now on they must find their own straw. But each day they must make just as many bricks as before."

So the people had to get straw wherever they could find it. It took a long time to gather stubble from the fields. And when they could not make as many bricks as before, the Hebrew foremen were beaten.

Then the Hebrew foremen came to Moses and Aaron and said, "You have made things worse than ever by going to the pharaoh. He says we do not have enough work to do. He says 'Make bricks!' but he does not give us any straw. And when we cannot make as many bricks as before, the Egyptians beat us."

Then Moses cried out to God, "Why did you ever send me? Ever since I came to Pharaoh to speak in your name, he has made things harder for us. You have not saved your people at all!"

But the Lord said to Moses, "Wait. You will see what I will do to Pharaoh. I am the Lord. I made a covenant with Abraham and with Isaac and with Jacob, and I will keep the promises that I made to them. Now tell the people of Israel that I will save them. I will take you for my people, and I will be your God; and I will bring you into the land which I promised to give to Abraham, to Isaac, and to Jacob. I will give you the land."

Moses told the people all that the Lord had said. But they did not want to listen anymore because they were afraid of the pharaoh.

GOD'S CONTEST WITH THE PHARAOH

The Lord said to Moses, "Go tell the pharaoh of Egypt to let the people of Israel go out of his land."

"If my own people will not listen to me, why will the pharaoh listen to me?" Moses objected.

Yet Moses did what the Lord commanded. Again Pharaoh would not listen. "Unless you prove by a sign that what you say about your God is true, I will not let the people go," he said.

So began a time of terrible plagues in Egypt. The River Nile turned as red as blood. The water became so poisoned

that fish died and there was no water fit to drink. Swarms of frogs, gnats, and flies spread over Egypt. They crawled and buzzed into the houses and food of the Egyptians and over their bodies. Cattle died of a strange disease, and people and animals were covered with terrible boils. Still the pharaoh refused to let the Hebrews go. Then hail beat down on fields and pasture lands—heavy hail that broke plants and grain. Swarms of locusts crawled and flew everywhere. They ate every plant and the fruit of every tree, so that nothing green remained in the fields.

Then a strange and terrifying darkness covered the land of the Egyptians. For three days they could not see anyone or anything. Finally the pharaoh ordered Moses to come to him and said, "Go, serve your God. Your children may go with you; but you must leave your flocks and herds behind."

But Moses said, "Our flocks and herds must go with us, for we will need them for making sacrifices to the Lord God."

Then the pharaoh became very angry and would not let the people go. "Get away from me," he said to Moses. "Do not let me see you again or I will have you put to death!"

Moses called together the chief men of the families of Israel and said: "Choose as many lambs for yourselves as each family can eat. Kill the lambs and catch the blood in a basin. Then take a bunch of hyssop and dip it into the blood and touch your doorposts and the beams over your doors with the blood. And none of you shall go out of his house until morning, for tonight the Lord will pass through to kill the firstborn of the Egyptians. But no harm will come to anyone whose house is marked with the blood of the lamb. This night the Lord will lead us out of Egypt. And when you come to the land which the Lord will give you, as he has promised, you shall celebrate a service as a remembrance of this night. And when your children ask you what it means, you shall say, 'It is the celebration of the Lord's passover, for he passed over the houses of the people of Israel in Egypt when he killed the Egyptians.'"

And the people of Israel bowed their heads and worshiped the Lord.

The Hebrew people obeyed Moses and marked their door-

posts and the beams over their doors with the blood of the lambs. In the long, dark hours of that night they packed their belongings in the flickering light of oil lamps. And the children watched with wondering eyes.

There was no death in the homes of the Hebrews, but it was a night of sorrow and pain for the families of Egypt. At midnight the oldest child in every Egyptian family died, from the firstborn of Pharaoh to the firstborn of the captive in the dungeon. There was not an Egyptian home in all the land where there was not weeping and sorrow.

Pharaoh called Moses and Aaron to him and said, "Leave

IN THE TIME OF MOSES

my land, you and your people. Go, serve your God. Take your flocks and your herds and be gone!"

Messengers hurried to tell all the Hebrews. They must gather families, animals, belongings, and food for the march out of Egypt. The Hebrews could not leave too quickly to please the Egyptians; they wanted to be rid of these people who had brought them so much trouble and pain!

Dough was lifted from the kneading bowls and bound up in cloaks to be baked on the way. Family belongings were slung over the backs of donkeys. Everyone and everything that walked carried a burden.

The terrible night of watching and waiting was over.

6. Moses and God's Victory

So on the Passover night the great journey out of Egypt began. They traveled slowly because they could not go faster than their flocks of sheep and their herds of cattle could walk. From the royal treasure city of Raamses south to Succoth, on to Etham at the edge of the wilderness the people journeyed. And God led them by day in a pillar of cloud and by night in a pillar of fire. At the edge of the great desert they stopped. And God told Moses to lead the people back to an open place by the Red Sea and to camp there.

The Israelites obeyed God and camped by the sea. And while they were there, the pharaoh changed his mind!

"What have we done!" Pharaoh said. "I cannot let these slaves escape from serving me."

So he got his chariot ready and ordered his soldiers and 600 of his best chariots and his best horsemen to come with him.

Swiftly they rode after the people of Israel. When the Hebrews saw the Egyptian army, they were very frightened.

"What have you done to us?" they shouted at Moses. "Did you bring us out of Egypt so that we might die here instead? It would have been better for us to serve the Egyptians than to die in the wilderness."

The whole camp was in an uproar. People stumbled over each other as they tried to gather up their belongings again. Mothers cried and clutched their children; fathers shouted for Moses to listen to them.

"But Moses said to the people, "Fear not, stand firm, and see the salvation which the Lord will work for you today. The Egyptians whom you see today you will never see again. The Lord will fight for you. You have only to be still."

Then the cloud in which God had led the people of Israel appeared behind them, separating them from the Egyptians. Moses stretched his hand out over the sea, and the Lord drove the sea back by a strong east wind all night long. So the people of Israel walked across where the water had been. The sun had not yet risen when the last of them crossed to the other side.

When the Egyptians saw what had happened, they drove their horses and chariots into the bed of the sea and tried one last time to capture the escaping Hebrew slaves. But the mud was soft and the wheels sank in deeply. Horses stumbled. Chariots and men weighted down with armor could not move. The Egyptians cried out to one another, "Let us go back. Surely the Lord fights for them!"

Then the Lord said to Moses, "Stretch out your hand over the sea." So Moses stretched out his hand, and the sea came back. The army of the pharaoh was trapped in the waters.

When the people saw what the Lord had done for them, they believed in him and trusted his servant Moses. They celebrated the victory of God and sang praises to him in songs like this one:

> I will sing to the LORD, for he has
>   triumphed gloriously;
> the horse and his rider he has
>   thrown into the sea.
>
> The LORD is my strength and my song,
>   and he has become my salvation;
> this is my God, and I will praise him,
>   my father's God, and I will exalt him.

IN THE TIME OF MOSES

Who is like thee, O LORD, among the gods?
Who is like thee, majestic in holiness,
    terrible in glorious deeds, doing wonders?

Thou hast led in thy steadfast love the
    people whom thou has redeemed,
thou hast guided them by thy strength to
    thy holy abode.

The LORD will reign forever and ever.

And always after that the Hebrews remembered how God had saved them from the Egyptians and led them out of slavery to be his people. They told the story over and over again to their children and to their children's children.

"The LORD brought us out of Egypt," they said, "with a mighty hand and an outstretched arm, with great terror, with signs and wonders."

Moses and God's Victory

7. Moses and God's Covenant Nation

"You have brought us into this wilderness to kill us all with hunger," the people complained to Moses.

They had dreamed of a grassy land "flowing with milk and honey." But instead they seemed lost in a waterless wilderness of scraggly bramble bushes and rocks and hot sun. The sacks that had held their food supplies were empty. The dough they had wrapped in their cloaks had been baked into bread and the last crumb eaten long ago. The goatskins that had carried their precious water lay flat and stiff.

Moses heard the people grumbling. He knew that many of them thought it would be better to go back to Egypt and be slaves again than to go on without food and water. Moses urged them on from one camping place to the next. Again and again he said, "Trust God! Believe that the Lord will keep his promise! God will bring you into the good land of Canaan!"

Just when the people were sure they could go no further, a flock of birds settled over their camp. Each evening more birds came. They were flocks of quail and very good to eat. And in the mornings the people found a strange white flaky food like frost on the ground. It tasted sweet, and they called it manna. In this way, God sent food to the people in the wilderness. But they did not stop complaining. Once when they could find no water, they blamed Moses and were almost ready to stone him to death! But God told Moses to hit the rocky side of the mountain with his staff. When he did, water gushed from the rocks. Now there were no thirsty or hungry travelers among the people.

MOUNT SINAI

In the third month after the people had left the land of Egypt, they came to a mountain called Sinai. Here they camped. It was a good spot. The great mountain protected their tents against strong winds. There was grass and water for sheep and cattle and level land for tents.

It was a spot that Moses knew well near the great mountain of God. Here he had tended his father-in-law's sheep. Here he had met God. Now God had kept his promise to bring him and his people back to the mountain.

GOD'S COVENANT WITH ISRAEL

After a time God spoke to Moses from the holy mountain and said, "Tell the people of Israel: You have seen what I did

Moses and God's Covenant Nation

IN THE TIME OF MOSES

Moses and God's Covenant Nation

to the Egyptians and how I . . . brought you to myself. Now therefore, if you will obey my voice and keep my covenant, you shall be my own." From all the nations of the earth, God had called the people of Israel to be his own nation and to worship and serve him only.

When the chief men of the people of Israel heard this, they answered, "All that God has spoken we will do."

On a special day the people came out of their tents and stood near the mountain. They trembled with excitement and fear. For God had announced that on this day he would come to them. It was morning, yet the light was more like the dim light of evening. There were thunder and lightning, but no rain. And the high peak of the mountain disappeared into a thick cloud.

Then a rumbling seemed to come from deep inside the mountain, and the earth began to shake. Some of the people pulled their cloaks over their faces. Some were afraid to look at the mountain. Children cried when thunder seemed to wrap itself around the mountain and jagged streaks of lightning sent sudden spears of white through the clouds.

A trumpet sounded. It grew louder and louder, cutting through the noise of the earthquake and the thunder and the cries of the trembling, fearful people. And God ordered Moses to come alone to the top of the mountain. The people stood far-off and waited.

When Moses returned, he had a solemn message. He told the people the words of God:

I am the LORD your God, who brought you out of the land of Egypt. . . . You shall have no other gods. . . .

You shall not take the name of the LORD your God in vain. . . .

Remember the sabbath day, to keep it holy. . . .

Honor your father and mother. . . .

You shall not kill.

You shall not commit adultery.

You shall not steal.

You shall not bear false witness against your neighbor.

You shall not covet. . . .

This is how Moses declared God's loving-kindness and brought God's laws to his people. They must obey these laws if they were to be God's people. The God who had shown his love for them by saving them from slavery now showed his love again by giving commandments to guide them in a good life.

And all the people said, "All the words which the LORD has spoken we will do."

Then they built an altar near the mountain, and set up twelve stone pillars, one for each tribe. The young men placed burnt offerings and sacrifices on the altar. These were a sign to tell God they they trusted him and wanted to be a God-fearing nation, apart from all other peoples.

Again Moses repeated the commandments and promises of God. And the people promised to obey God, their King.

Now Israel belonged to God. He had made a covenant with them. He was their God; they were his people.

BROKEN PROMISES

Then God commanded Moses, "Come up to me on the mountain, and wait there; and I will tell you all that I want you to do."

So Moses went up on the mountain alone. Aaron was to be in charge while he was gone. Every day the people looked to the mountain to see if Moses were coming back. But long days stretched into longer weeks and still Moses did not return. At last they began to wonder if he would ever come back.

"We do not know what has become of Moses," they said. "Perhaps he has gone to live at the top of the mountain and will never come back to lead us out of this wilderness."

The people felt very much alone, so they turned to Aaron. "Make us gods to lead us," they demanded.

IN THE TIME OF MOSES

Then Aaron told them to bring the golden earrings they had brought from Egypt. He melted the gold and molded it into the shape of a bull like the idols of Egypt. When the golden statue was finished, the people shouted, "This is our god who brought us out of the land of Egypt!" But the idol was small and it was called the golden calf.

MOSES COMES BACK

Then Moses came down from the mountaintop. He carried two tablets of stone on which were carved the commandments of God. He heard the noise of singing near the camp. And when he saw the little golden idol and the people dancing around it, his anger burned hot and he hurled the tablets to the ground, smashing them at the foot of the mountain.

Moses seized the little golden calf and threw it into the fire. Then he ground it into powder and mixed it with water and made the people drink it. Moses had not thought that the people would so quickly forget all that God had done for them and the promises they had made to the Lord.

Moses turned to Aaron. "What made you do this thing?"

Aaron shook with fear. "Do not be angry with me. The people made me do it. They said to me, 'Make us gods to lead us, for we do not know what has happened to Moses.' So I told them to bring their gold and I threw it in the fire, and this calf came out!"

Moses shouted to the people, "You have sinned a great sin." And the people were filled with grief and fear.

Then Moses climbed up to the mountain peak and prayed, "O Lord, these people have sinned a great sin. We are a proud and stubborn people, who want our own way more than we want yours. But if I have found favor with you, O Lord, stay with us and be our God, even though we do not deserve your kindness. Pardon our sin, and take us back to be your holy nation again."

God forgave Israel and renewed his covenant with them. And Moses carved the commandments of God on tablets of stone again.

FORTY YEARS IN THE WILDERNESS

For forty years the people of Israel lived in the wilderness, learning how God wanted them to live. They herded their flocks and wandered from oasis to oasis. They made a tent of beautiful cloth in colors of blue and purple and scarlet. Over it they spread a strong tent of goat hair and leather to protect it from sun and weather. They called this holy place "The Tabernacle," and here they came to worship.

And they made a chest of fine wood and covered it with gold. They placed inside it the tablets of God's commandments and called the chest the "Ark of the Covenant." And wherever the people of Israel went, the priests led the way, carrying the Ark on long poles. The Ark was a sign and a reminder that God was with them.

Early in the forty years in the wilderness, God brought his people to the edge of the land of Canaan. But the people

IN THE TIME OF MOSES

were afraid to cross over into the land. They feared the people of Canaan and the thick, strong walls around their cities. Again the people complained, saying, "The Lord hates us; he has brought us here to destroy us!"

Once more Moses reminded the people how God had brought them out of Egypt and protected them on the long journey. "The Lord will fight for you," he said. "Do not be afraid."

But the people did not trust God that much, so the Lord would not let them enter the land. Instead they turned back and lived in the wilderness the rest of their lives. Most of the grown men and women who left Egypt never saw the Promised Land.

THE PROMISED LAND

Finally when the children and grandchildren were grown up, the people were ready to cross the Jordan River into Canaan. By then Moses was very old. He knew that God would not allow him to lead the people into the land. So he chose Joshua to take his place.

For the last time Moses gathered all the people. He spoke solemnly to Joshua, "Be strong and of good courage; for you shall go with this people into the land which the LORD has sworn to their fathers. . . . It is the LORD who goes before you; he will be with you, he will not fail you . . . do not fear."

Then Moses said to the people, "Remember that you belong to God. Because God loved you, he chose you to be his

people. You must remember always how he saved you from the land of Egypt and led you through the wilderness. And now he is bringing you into a good land. This is the land he promised to your fathers, to Abraham, to Isaac, and to Jacob. You must fear the Lord your God, and walk in his ways, and love him. You must serve him with your whole heart and keep his commandments. If you do these things, the Lord will bless you and your descendants in the land he will give you. If you do not do

these things, then you will surely perish."

Then Moses climbed to the top of Mount Nebo, and there the Lord showed him all the land of Canaan.

Moses died, and Joshua led the people into Canaan. But never again was there a leader in Israel like Moses. He was the faithful servant whom God had chosen to bring his people out of slavery and to help them be a holy nation under the Lord.

Moses and God's Covenant Nation 71

Part 3

A King for
God's People

8. David, Israel's Favorite King

The long hard years in the wilderness were over. A new life was beginning for God's people. They had come at last to the promised land of Canaan; this was to be their home.

But if the people of Israel thought their troubles were over, they were wrong. Before they could settle down in the new land, they had to fight to win it from the people who already lived there. Sometimes the people of Canaan let them settle peacefully near their towns and fields. More often the Israelites fought bloody battles to capture a city or a rich valley. Joshua was a wise and brave army leader and a good planner. But it was a long time before the people of Israel could win enough battles so they could say the land was really theirs. Even then there were some cities which they could not capture. And they did not dare go near the land at the shore of the Great Sea where the strong warrior Philistines lived.

A KING FOR GOD'S PEOPLE

When the tribes of Israel came into the land of Canaan, they had to learn new things. They had to learn to build houses and settle down in towns and villages. This was hard for them because all their lives they had lived in tents and moved about in the wilderness as they pleased with their flocks. Now they had to learn all that a farmer needs to know to plow and plant, to sow and reap. They had to learn to live with their Canaanite neighbors. And all the while they had to protect their land from enemy raiders from the desert.

A PEOPLE WHO FORGOT

The biggest problem of all was remembering to live as God's people. The people of Canaan worshiped many gods. They prayed to gods of harvest and gods of sun and rain. They called their gods Baals. Baal means Lord. To the Israelites the name was like the one they used—the Lord God. It was easier to worship these gods of Canaan than to worship the Lord God. The Baals did not make a lot of rules for the way you must live.

In the years in the land of Canaan the people of Israel no longer remembered the God who had led their fathers out of Egypt through the wilderness and given them the land of Canaan. Instead they began to worship the false gods of their neighbors. They even forgot they were one nation. Instead each tribe did what it pleased. Each tribe had to fight off its enemies alone. Often a tribe was defeated and had to give up part of its land or let raiders take away the harvest.

But even though the people of Israel had forgotten God, God did not forget them. When times were very hard and the tribes prayed for help, God gave them strong leaders called judges. The judges helped the tribes fight their enemies. Often the judges reminded the people that they belonged to the Lord God. The judges repeated the promises of God to make them a great nation which would bring his blessing to all the world. For a while the people would try to obey God. But when a judge died, the people would often forget God again.

WE WANT A KING!

The Philistines were getting stronger and bolder. They marched inland from their cities along the coast and tried to take the land away from the Israelites. The Philistines were good fighters, and many times they defeated the people of Israel. Once they even stole the Ark of the Covenant! But they sent it back. They thought it brought them bad luck. The Philistines even built forts in the hills in the center of Canaan. If something did not happen soon to help Israel, they would lose the land they had fought so hard to win.

In those days there lived a judge named Samuel. All the tribes of Israel knew that Samuel was a great and wise man of God. He was a priest and a judge who spoke to the people for God. So the tribes of Israel sent men to Samuel, saying, "We need a king. The other nations are strong because they have kings. We must have a king to rule over all our tribes, or we will lose our land."

A KING FOR GOD'S PEOPLE

At first Samuel did not like their idea. "We are not like other nations," he reminded them. "We are God's chosen people. God is our king."

The people would not listen to Samuel. "We want a king!" they shouted. "We are going to have a king!"

So God told Samuel to choose a man from the tribe of Benjamin to be king over God's people. The man God chose was Saul. Saul was very strong and tall and handsome. He was a brave soldier and a good leader. And he was faithful to God. No wonder the people cheered their new king!

The people were glad, but Samuel warned them: "If both you and the king who rules over you will follow the Lord your God, everything will be well. But if you do not listen to God, and if you do not do what God tells you, then the Lord will be against you and your king."

A KING WHO FAILED

When he first became king, Saul asked God to guide him in everything he did. He even made his battle plans according to what he believed God commanded. Samuel had told him, "The king must be God's servant." And Saul believed Samuel.

Saul won victory after victory. He turned Israel's enemies back, and some he defeated. Surely God was leading his people! Before every battle Saul tried to find out what God commanded. But in time of war this became very hard to do. Sometimes Saul quickly made up his own mind instead of waiting until he was sure he knew what God wanted. And sometimes, even when he knew what God wanted him to do, he chose his own way instead.

During one war Saul disobeyed an order of God that Samuel had given him. Then Samuel, God's priest who spoke for God, told Saul, "You can no longer be God's chosen servant." Saul had failed to give God the one thing God demanded of a king—complete obedience.

Even after he knew that God was no longer with him, Saul had to go on being king. His followers still thought he was the mightiest hero in the land and the bravest soldier.

A KING FOR GOD'S PEOPLE

But now Saul was an unhappy man. Samuel no longer came to give advice and help. Saul missed his wise old friend. He would think of how he had failed God, and he felt alone and afraid. He was not afraid of enemies or battles. But Saul was afraid because he did not feel sure anymore that God was with him. Sometimes he would sit by himself and refuse to talk to anyone. Other times he shouted in anger at everyone.

One day a servant who loved Saul said, "I know a young man who is good at playing the lyre. He is a fine-looking man, brave and intelligent. He is a good soldier, and the Lord is with him. Let us bring him here. Whenever you are sad or frightened, he will play for you, and you will be well."

The name of that young man was David, the son of Jesse. And Saul sent messengers to find him.

DAVID IN THE KING'S COURT

David, the youngest son of Jesse, was herding sheep when Saul's messengers arrived at his home in Bethlehem. He came in from the fields and stood before them. His hair was blown by the summer winds. His skin was browned by the sun. And when he laughed, his eyes sparkled.

"The king will be pleased to have such a good-looking young lad near him," the messengers agreed. "With the laughter and music of David to cheer him, perhaps he will get well."

David's father was pleased, too. He knew something about David that the messengers did not know. He knew that God had chosen David to be the next king. Samuel had come and anointed David as a sign that he was chosen by God. So David's father sent bread and wine and a young goat from his flocks as gifts to Saul, and David left his home in Bethlehem to enter the service of the king.

Soon David's music filled the royal house. How simply and easily his fingers plucked the strings of his lyre! He sang as he had done when he watched his father's sheep. Often he sang songs of praise to God.

And Saul was comforted by David's music and by the strength of his faith. And he loved him greatly.

DAVID, THE PEOPLE'S HERO

David soon became more than court musician and poet. He was a brave soldier, and Saul made him his armor bearer. The king's son Jonathan became David's best friend. As a sign of their friendship, the young prince gave David his robe and his armor, and even his sword and bow. So David was like a son to Saul and a brother to Jonathan.

Then Saul made the brave young David a captain in his army. David was a good leader, and his men loved him and followed him faithfully. No matter what enemies David fought, he always won. It seemed that Saul's armies could not lose when David led them! Everywhere he went the people cheered him as a hero. When he came riding back from his victories, the women of Israel came out of the cities along the way, singing and dancing and playing songs of praise to David, "Saul has slain his thousands and David his *ten* thousands!"

A KING FOR GOD'S PEOPLE

The song was true, and King Saul knew it. The same young man he had brought to his house to comfort and calm him now made him more afraid and angry than before. Saul knew that he had lost God's favor. He could not stand the thought that he was losing the favor of his people, too. He did not want David to be their hero. He became insanely jealous.

"What more can he want now but the kingdom?" cried Saul. In his heart he knew that some day David would be king—unless something happened to stop it. Saul made up his mind that David must not live long enough to be king!

David knew how jealous Saul was. "There is only one step between me and death," he told his friend Jonathan. "Your father will not be satisfied until he kills me."

David, Israel's Favorite King

So David left the royal house that had been his home. And Jonathan, who loved David very much, promised to let him know in three days whether or not it was safe to return.

"Hide in the field outside the city gate," Jonathan told David. "On the third day I will shoot some arrows. If I tell the boy who is with me, 'Look, the arrows are on this side of you,' then it will be safe for you to come back. But if I say, 'Look, the arrows went past you,' then you must run!"

On the second day that David was gone, Saul said to Jonathan, "Where is Jesse's son? He was not at dinner yesterday or today!"

"David asked me for permission to go to Bethlehem to see his brothers," Jonathan answered, "and I told him it was all right."

Then Saul was very angry because Jonathan had helped David. "As long as the son of Jesse is alive, you will never be king!" he shouted. "Now send for him and bring him to me, for he shall surely die."

Jonathan could not believe that the father he loved really meant to kill his friend. "Why should he be put to death?" he asked. "What has he done?"

Saul seized his spear and flung it at Jonathan. Then Jonathan was sure that his father really meant to kill David.

The next morning he took his arrows and went to the field outside the city gates. He said to the little boy who was with him, "Run and find the arrows which I shoot." As the boy started to run, Jonathan shot an arrow past him and called, "Look, the arrow went past you. Hurry!" It was the signal that David should run for his life.

The two young men could not bear to leave one another without saying good-bye. So Jonathan sent the boy back to the city alone, and David came from his hiding place behind a heap of stones. And the two friends wept because they knew they might never see each other again.

A HUNTED MAN

From that day on David was a hunted man. Now he could not go back to the king's court or lead the king's army. And he was never safe from Saul, who followed him with his soldiers and tried many times to kill him. So David became an outlaw.

In the cave of Adullam, David hid with his own fighting men. His brothers and his father's family and servants joined him. And anyone who was hungry or in debt or unhappy with the way King Saul ruled the country gathered there, too. For several years David hid from King Saul.

In the city of Ziklag in the south of Canaan, David was waiting for news from Saul's camp. A hundred miles to the north at Mount Gilboa, Israel's armies were fighting a great and bloody battle against their old enemies, the powerful Philistines.

At last a messenger arrived. "The armies of Saul are beaten!" he shouted. "The men have fled from the battle.

Saul and Jonathan are dead." The messenger was eager to tell David that his days of hiding in dark, cold caves were over and that he need fear Saul no longer. Perhaps David could now become king!

When David heard the messenger, he turned his face away and wept. There were no shouts of joy in David's camp and no cheers for freedom. And David went to be alone and weep that Jonathan, his dearest friend, was dead.

ISRAEL'S GREATEST KING

Not long after Saul's death, David did become king of all Israel. At first he was crowned king only of the tribe of Judah in the south. Finally he was crowned king of all the tribes.

And what a king David became! He moved swiftly to build a great and enduring kingdom. In those days the great city of Jerusalem did not belong to Israel. It was a separate city built on a hill and protected by mighty walls. No one had been able to capture it; no one believed that it ever could be captured. No one—except David! The new king wanted to capture Jerusalem and make it his capital city. So David brought his soldiers to the city walls. Secretly he sent picked men into the city through an underground tunnel from a spring and captured the city from the inside, by surprise.

King David made Jerusalem the most important city in Israel. Here he built a beautiful palace. From here he led his soldiers into battle against the Philistines and drove Israel's old enemies out of the land forever.

How proud the people were of their brave soldier king! From one end of the country to the other, people told the stories of David's great victories.

More than ever before, the people of Israel were united as one nation. And the land—the Promised Land—was now truly their own. David's kingdom grew larger and larger as his armies defeated the lands to the east and south. Then there was a time of peace. Caravans brought cedar logs and bronze and gold for building David's palace. And the king grew in power and riches.

SERVANT OF GOD

David remembered that the real king of Israel was God. He did not forget that any king in Israel must be God's servant. He must first of all do what God commands. David wanted his people to remember that they were God's people. So he made Jerusalem the place where people should come to make sacrifices to God and worship him. David also ordered the Ark of the Covenant brought to Jerusalem. People had almost forgotten the old Ark, but David wanted his people to remember always that God was still leading his people just as he had led them through the wilderness long ago.

On the day when the Ark was carried to Jerusalem, there was a great celebration. David himself led the singing procession through the streets. On this day the king did not ride in a royal chair so that his people could cheer him. Instead he came on foot, showing his gladness by leaping and dancing in front of

A KING FOR GOD'S PEOPLE

the Ark. And he told his people to blow trumpets and play music and sing songs of praise to God, their mighty King.

David made other plans for a wonderful temple to be built in Jerusalem.

"It is not right," he said, "that I should live in a house made of cedar while the Ark of God is in a tent." But David could only begin to make plans for a temple. Many years later, David's son Solomon would finally build the temple his father had dreamed of.

When David was king, he thought of the day long ago when God had called him from the fields and told him he was to be king over his people. He thought of all the wonderful things God had done for him and for Israel.

And David prayed: "I do not deserve such great love. How can I thank you, God? What can I say? Because you loved us, you have done all these things! You have kept the promises you made to our fathers, to Abraham and Isaac and Jacob. Therefore you are great, O Lord God, for there is no one like you; there is no God besides you. What other nation on earth is like your people Israel? You took them out of Egypt; you made them a nation and became their God. I am your servant, O Lord God. Bless me and my house, that we may serve you forever!"

DAVID'S GREAT SIN

But even the great King David sometimes failed God. In the spring of the year, a time when kings go forth to battle,

David sent his general Joab to lead the soldiers. And King David stayed in his palace in Jerusalem.

Late one afternoon, when David was walking on the roof of his house, he saw a beautiful woman in a neighbor's garden. Her name was Bathsheba. David wanted her to be his wife. But Bathsheba was already married to Uriah, a soldier in David's army. So David sent a letter to Joab. "Put Uriah in the front line where the fighting is hardest," the letter said.

Joab obeyed his king's command. And Uriah was killed in battle. Then David brought Bathsheba to his house and she became his wife. But the thing that David had done did not please God.

God sent Nathan the prophet to David, and Nathan spoke to David for God. He told the king a story:

"There were two men in a certain city. One was rich and the other poor. The rich man had many flocks and herds, but the poor man had only one little lamb. And the poor man loved his lamb. One day a traveler came to visit the rich man. The rich man did not want to take one of his own animals to prepare for dinner, so he took the poor man's lamb instead."

When David heard the story, he was very angry. "The man who has done this deserves to die!" he said.

Then Nathan said to David, "You are the man!"

And David knew then that he was like the rich man in the story, for he had murdered Uriah and taken his wife from him.

"Thus says the Lord," continued Nathan, "I have anointed you king over Israel, and I kept you from being killed by Saul.

Why have you turned against me to do what is evil in my sight?"

"I have sinned against the Lord," cried David. And he wept for the wrong he had done. For he knew that his sin was not just a sin against Uriah but a sin against God.

Then Nathan said to the king, "Because you are truly sorry and seek forgiveness, the Lord has put away your sin. You shall not die."

David knew he deserved to die because he had sent Uriah to his death. David had turned away from God. But God had not turned away from him. God's love was great enough to forgive him and save him from death. So David returned to God and prayed that God would help him obey his law.

"Have mercy on me, O God, according to thy
    steadfast love;
according to thy abundant mercy blot out
    my transgressions.
Wash me thoroughly from my iniquity,
    and cleanse me from my sin!

Create in me a clean heart, O God,
    and put a new and right spirit within me.
Cast me not away from thy presence,
    and take not thy holy Spirit from me.
Restore to me the joy of thy salvation,
    and uphold me with a willing spirit."

In the long years after the time of King David, the people hoped that someday God would send them another king just like David. No one thought that someday God would send his own Son to be born where David was born—in the village of Bethlehem.

But it was not yet time for that to happen.

9. Solomon, Israel's Richest King

Shopkeepers in the streets of Jerusalem passed the exciting news from door to door: "The Queen of Sheba is on her way to visit our King Solomon!" Housewives chattered together as they ground flour and baked bread in their outdoor ovens. "Is she really as beautiful as everyone says?"

Everywhere people were talking: "Why is she coming? Perhaps she has heard of our king's great wisdom and wants to ask him questions." Stonecutters and carpenters wondered what the queen would think of the grand, new buildings they had helped to build. Children playing in Jerusalem's streets played that they were the royal caravan bringing the famous queen to see Solomon, David's son. Swiftly the news was carried to every corner of the beautiful, busy city.

Who would have thought the day would come when kings and queens would come from other lands to see Israel's king! It was not many years ago that the great king David died. But if he could see Jerusalem now he would scarcely recognize it. Everywhere there were new and beautiful buildings, magnificent palaces, rich decorations of silver and ivory and gold. From far away the ships of Solomon brought back gold and rich spices, apes and peacocks, ivory and precious stones. Rich visitors to the king brought gifts of fine cloth, myrrh and gold, horses and mules. It was a time of peace and plenty.

The temple that David had dreamed of was finished. It was made of polished white stone that shone like the rays of of the sun. The walls and ceiling were lined with carved cedar. Gold was used to cover the cypress floors and walls of the dark and holy room where the Ark of the Covenant stood. The beautiful temple was meant to be a sign that the people trusted in God. Here priests brought sacrifices to God each day and temple choirs sang songs of praise. People came from all parts of the kingdom of Israel to worship God. The temple had become the most important place in all Israel.

The fame of Solomon, the rich and wise king, spread to many lands. Visitors came from far away to the city of Jerusalem to see its beauty and to hear the wisdom of the king. And now the famous queen was coming, too.

THE QUEEN OF SHEBA

The day of the great queen's arrival was a day Israel long remembered. Other caravans had come through the city before, but no caravan had been like this one! Court musicians announced the queen's entrance into the city. With her came a long procession. There were camels bearing spices and carved chests filled with gold and precious stones. There were soldiers and officials, ladies-in-waiting and hairdressers, musicians and dancers. And the queen herself, beautiful to see, was carried through the streets in great honor.

The Queen of Sheba was amazed by all she saw in Israel's famous city. Stonecutters were shaping great blocks for new buildings. Foremen shouted directions to workers pulling ropes to set up great pillars. Carpenters were sawing costly lumber from the faraway forests of Lebanon and Ophir. Careful woodworkers were carving beautiful designs in the fine wood.

In the royal palace King Solomon himself waited to greet the queen and welcome her with all the splendor of his kingdom. His great throne was made of ivory and decorated with gold. The back of the throne was carved like the head of a calf, and a carved lion stood at each side of the arms of the chair. Twelve carved lions, one at each end of the six steps, guarded the way to the throne.

In the long dining hall built with beams of cedar, the queen was guest of honor at great banquets. She marveled at the fine food, the sweet fruits, and many dishes of meat and vegetables. She drank rare wines from gold goblets. The great queen enjoyed all the many wonders of Solomon's rich and splendid kingdom.

The queen had heard how wise Solomon was. She brought many hard questions to test the king, and Solomon could answer every one of them. So the queen said, "In my own land I heard of your riches and your wisdom. But I did not believe the stories until I came and saw for myself. Now I know that you are even wiser than people say you are."

"When I first became king after the death of my father David," Solomon told her, "I had a dream. In my dream God told me to ask for whatever I wanted him to give me. I asked for wisdom to understand and rule my people well and to know what is right. And God gave me a wise and understanding mind. He also gave me what I did not ask for—riches and honor. All that you see, and all that I have, and all that Israel has become is God's gift."

The queen asked many questions about the God King Solomon served, and she learned how God had brought the Hebrew people into the Promised Land. Before she left, she said to King Solomon, "Blessed be the Lord your God, who has favored you and set you on the throne of Israel. Because the Lord loved Israel forever, he has made you king, that you may do what is right and rule with justice."

Then she gave the king a large treasure of gold and more spices and precious stones than anyone had ever brought to Israel before.

And Solomon was known far and wide for his wisdom and his riches and his desire to serve the Lord.

A KING FOR GOD'S PEOPLE

To the visiting queen everything in Israel seemed right and good. Yet there was much that was wrong in Solomon's kingdom. There were wrongs which would bring sorrow and trouble to the land. Solomon's new buildings were handsome, but much gold and labor was needed to build them. Gold was needed to send ships to bring back precious metals and jewels from faraway lands. Soldiers and laborers were needed for the big army and for building new cities. And the people had to pay for all of this!

Every year the king demanded more taxes. People grumbled: "When will it all stop? Did our fathers fight for this land just so that we could work and pay to dress and feed our splendid king?"

Some of the old men would answer, "It is all part of God's plan. To have a king, we must have a city fit for a king."

But many thought the city was already fine enough. "Our king wants too much," they said.

Solomon had prayed to know what was right and to rule his people fairly. But was it right to make his people pay high taxes to build his palaces and cities? Was it fair to make them work in labor gangs so that Jerusalem would be famous as a rich and splendid city? Was it right to force people to work as slaves on his big and expensive projects? Was this what God wanted?

More and more people did not think so.

Something else was not right about the way King Solomon was leading God's people. As time went by, King Solomon made friendly agreements with many countries. Each time he married a princess of that land. Soon he had many wives. Each time a new wife came to live in the palace, she brought along her own gods. And the king allowed his wives to build altars in Jerusalem to worship their gods. Soon Solomon was worshiping these false gods himself!

Solomon had forgotten that the king must be God's servant. He had forgotten the promise that God had made long ago to Abraham: "I will make you a great nation, and your descendants will bring my blessing to all the world!" The king over God's people was leading them away from God!

Part 4

In the Time of the Prophets

10. *Jeremiah and the End of a Kingdom*

In the years of King Solomon the kingdom was at peace. And when the king died, the crown of David was placed on the head of Rehoboam, the son of Solomon. Now at last, the people hoped, life would be easier. They hoped that young King Rehoboam would not order them to serve in his work gangs or to give more money for rich palaces as Solomon had done.

But Rehoboam made things harder than ever for God's people. "My father made you pay high taxes," he said, "but I will make them higher. My father made you work hard for him, but I will make you work harder." Rehoboam wanted to have a splendid kingdom.

When the men of the north heard this, they were angry. For years they had given from their harvests to King Solomon. They had worked to build the king's buildings. Each year they had had to pay greater taxes. They were tired of giving up so much for a city so far away. So the men of the north chose their own king and made their own kingdom.

Now instead of one kingdom, there were two. The large one in the north was called Israel; the small one in the south around Jerusalem was called Judah. The great kingdom that Saul and David had worked so hard to make into one nation was split in two.

THE END OF ISRAEL

For a while the men of Israel in the north came to the Temple in Jerusalem to worship God. This was the place where the Ark of the Covenant was kept and the place where they thought God lived. But when the king of Israel saw the people going to Jerusalem to worship, he was afraid.

"This will have to stop," he thought. "If my people go down to Jerusalem to worship, they may turn away from me and return to the kingdom of Judah."

And so the king of Israel built two small temples, one in the far north of his kingdom and one in the south. In each temple he placed a statue of a calf. Then he said to the people, "These are your gods who brought you up out of the land of Egypt. Do not go to Jerusalem to worship, but bring your offerings here."

This was the way the king led the people of Israel astray. After a time the people said, "What difference does it make if we worship the Lord God and also the Baals of Canaan?" Some could not tell the difference between a Baal and the true

God. And so they turned to worship false gods, and wicked kings led the people farther and farther away from the Lord God. Even the kings forgot the covenant God had made with his people. And so the people forgot the Lord God who had chosen them to be his people and to serve him.

In those days God sent men to tell the people that they belonged to him, to teach the people about God, and to warn them that if they did not listen to God, they would be destroyed. These men were prophets. God sent the prophet Elijah, who lived in the wilderness and wore a coat of rough camel's hair.

And in later years God sent Amos, a shepherd from the hills of Tekoa, to tell the people of Israel that God is holy and therefore the people must give up their wrongdoing and do what is right and true. But the people would not listen and the king of Israel sent Amos away.

God sent other prophets, too. He sent Hosea to tell the people that God still loved them, even though they had done evil, and that he was waiting to take them back if only they would come back to him.

But the men of Israel were rich and happy, and they would not believe the prophets of God. Not until the mighty armies of Assyria tramped across their fields from the north, did they remember the words of the prophets. But then it was too late. The Assyrians burned the cities of Israel and took the people away to be slaves. And they were never heard of again.

Now the kingdom of Israel was no more. Of the people of God, only the little kingdom of Judah was left.

There was trouble, too, in the kingdom of Judah. Sometimes wicked kings built altars and temples to false gods. One king even put up idols in the Temple in Jerusalem for people to worship! And when some of the men of Judah spoke out against the terrible thing the king had done, the king ordered them put to death.

But sometimes Judah had a good king who tried to do what was right. When that happened, the temples and altars to false gods came tumbling down. The king ordered the idols to be broken in pieces and ground into dust. And the good king reminded the people that if they did not keep their promises to God, they would lose everything God had given them.

Then the people returned to God and tried to obey him. They tried to live as he wanted them to live. They taught their children the old stories about how God had saved them from slavery and brought them to the promised land of Canaan. They told stories of the great King David, who loved God and wanted the people to remember that they were God's people and that God had a wonderful plan for them.

One of the good kings was Josiah. He was trying to help Judah live as God's people when new trouble came. Egypt's armies were getting ready to attack another strong nation, Babylonia—and little Judah was in the way! Brave King Josiah went to war to stop the Egyptian armies from marching through Judah. Josiah fought a great battle against

the Egyptians, but the Egyptians defeated the men of Judah and killed King Josiah. After the battle, Egypt chose a new king to rule over Judah. This king's name was Jehoiakim. And Jehoiakim did not love God.

Soon Egypt's gods and Egypt's ways were brought into Judah. Temples and altars to false gods were set up again. And the ways of God were forgotten in Judah.

In those years false prophets pretended to speak for God, but they only told the people lies. Babylonia was growing stronger. Many people in Judah were worried that the Babylonians might destroy their kingdom just as Assyria had destroyed Israel.

The false prophets and priests kept saying, "God will not destroy his own house. The Temple will keep all of us safe." They did not tell the people to trust God; they only said, "Trust the Temple." They did not think it was important to obey God in everything they did. They thought that because the Temple of God was in Jerusalem, nothing bad could happen to them.

GOD CALLS A PROPHET

In the village of Anathoth in Judah lived a young man named Jeremiah. His father was a priest. Jeremiah had often heard the stories of God's covenant with his people. He loved the land of Judah, and he did not like to see his people worshiping other gods. How long would God be patient with his people when they refused to serve and obey him? Jeremiah was sure that if the people did not change, Judah would lose the land God had given them.

Then God called Jeremiah to do a very hard thing. "You must speak for me to the kingdom of Judah," he told Jeremiah. "You must tell the king and the people that because they have not obeyed me, they will be destroyed."

Jeremiah was afraid, and he said to God, "But I do not know how to speak well enough. I am too young!"

But God said, "Do not say you are too young. To whomever I send you, you shall go; and whatever I command you, you shall speak. Do not be afraid, for I am with you. Men will fight against you, but I am with you and I will save you."

JEREMIAH SPEAKS FOR GOD

So Jeremiah went to Jerusalem as God commanded him. People from all the cities of Judah had come to the Temple for a festival. And Jeremiah stood in the Temple courtyard:

"Hear the words of the Lord!" he said. "You must change your ways, or you will not be saved! Do not trust the priests who tell you that the Temple will save you. It will not. The Lord wants his people to obey him. But you are not fair to each other; you are not kind to your neighbors; you murder and steal and lie and commit adultery. You turn your backs on God and worship gods who are no gods. And then you come here to the Lord's Temple and expect him to save you!

"Therefore God is going to destroy you, and you will not be able to escape. Jerusalem will fall to your enemies, and

Jeremiah and the End of a Kingdom 109

the Temple where you do not worship God will crumble in ruins. The king will be taken from his throne. And when people pass by and ask why the Lord has let this happen to his great city, then you must answer, 'Because we did not obey the voice of the Lord our God.' "

What Jeremiah said made the king and the priests and the people very angry. They did not like what Jeremiah said, and they did not want to believe his words. Instead they wanted to kill Jeremiah. But they were afraid to kill a prophet because he said he spoke for God. So they let him go and told him to stay away from the Temple. The guards had orders: keep this troublesome prophet out of the Temple!

Jeremiah became a lonely and hated man. Even his own family would have nothing to do with him. How he wished he could make his people hear what God was trying to say to them! How he wished he could make them come back to God before it was too late! But the people only laughed at him. Some thought he must be crazy. Others called him a traitor and said that he hated his country!

Sometimes Jeremiah felt so tired and discouraged and lonely that he wanted to give up. Then God helped him to be strong again and speak boldly to the people.

THE CLAY JAR

Jeremiah looked for new ways to make the people listen to God. One day he saw a potter shaping a lump of clay. He pushed and smoothed the clay as his wheel spun faster and faster. But the clay did not turn into the beautiful jar the potter wanted to make, so the potter squeezed the clay back into a lump and started all over again.

As Jeremiah watched the potter work, an idea from God came to him. "Judah is just like that clay," he thought. "God wants to make Judah into a fine, great nation, but Judah does not want to be the kind of nation God wants it to be. God will destroy Judah, just as the potter had to destroy his clay jar."

When Jeremiah told his story to the people, they said, "That is foolish! We will not listen to you."

JEREMIAH'S SCROLL

Then God gave Jeremiah another idea. Since he was not allowed to speak to the people, he could write down God's message. Jeremiah called his friend Baruch, a scribe. As Jeremiah spoke, Baruch wrote down each word on a scroll. When the scroll was finished, Jeremiah said, "The gates of the Temple are closed to me. But you can go into the Temple and read the scroll to the people. Perhaps then they will listen to my words and will turn from their evil ways and trust and obey God."

So Baruch went into the city on a day when many people were at the Temple. And Baruch stood in the upper court where everyone could see and hear him, and he read the scroll of Jeremiah. One of the men who listened was a servant in the palace of the king. When he heard Baruch read the words of Jeremiah, he ran to the king's palace with the news.

Jeremiah and the End of a Kingdom   III

The princes of Judah had gathered in the king's palace. They sent a man named Jehudi to bring Baruch and his scroll to them.

And they said to Baruch, "Sit down and read the scroll to us."

When they had heard Baruch read, they asked, "How did you write all these words? Did Jeremiah tell you what to write?"

And Baruch answered, "Yes."

Then the princes said to Baruch, "You are in great danger. You and Jeremiah must hide. Do not tell anyone where you are."

Then Jehudi took the scroll and read it to the king. It was winter, and the king sat by a small stove, warming himself at the fire. When he heard the words of Jeremiah warning that Jerusalem and all of Judah would be destroyed, the king was furious. And when he heard the words that told of the evil of the king and the people, he was even more angry. As Jehudi read the scroll, King Jehoiakim reached out with his penknife and slashed off part of the scroll. Into the fire it went! Jehudi read more, and more was slashed off and burned. King Jehoiakim did not want to hear the truth about himself and his country.

And so the scroll of Jeremiah was destroyed. But this did not stop Jeremiah. His words were not forgotten, for Jeremiah repeated all of the message of God and Baruch wrote it again on a new scroll.

THE WOODEN YOKE

A time of trouble began just as Jeremiah had said it would. The armies of Babylonia marched into Judah. They broke through the walls of Jerusalem. Soldiers burst into the palace and captured King Jehoiakim and all his family. They took thousands of the most important people of Judah to Babylonia to be slaves. They raided the Temple and carried away all the gold and silver and everything of value. They left the city of Jerusalem standing, but it was no longer the proud city it had been before.

Jeremiah stayed in Jerusalem. God had work for him to do, but now it was even harder than before. Jeremiah must tell Judah's new king, Zedekiah, that the people of Judah must serve the king of Babylonia and not fight against him. To make sure Zedekiah understood what Judah was supposed to do, Jeremiah acted out God's message. He made a yoke like the wooden bar a team of oxen wore for pulling a plow or a cart. And he put this heavy yoke on his own neck! This was a sign that God wanted Judah to serve Babylonia as oxen serve their master.

This message of Jeremiah was hard to believe! Did God really want his people to serve the cruel king of Babylonia who had taken away many of their relatives and friends to be his slaves?

"Yes!" answered Jeremiah. "This is God's way to punish Judah for not obeying him. Serve the king of Babylonia and you will live. Babylonia's rule will last a long time. But someday God will bring his people back. God will not forget us, and he will keep his promises."

But no one wanted to believe Jeremiah.

LETTERS OF HOPE AND COMFORT

Then God showed Jeremiah what he would do for his people. For many years they must live in the faraway city called Babylon. But God would not forget his people. He would forgive them. Someday he would bring them back to Jerusalem.

Jeremiah wrote long letters to God's people in Babylon. He wrote, "Trust God! Do not forget your Lord! Pray to the

Lord God and serve him, even though you are far away from home. God will hear your prayers. He will help you." This message was hard for the people to understand; they thought they could worship God only in the Temple in Jerusalem. Now they were learning that God was with them in the strange city of Babylon, too.

Jeremiah had preached God's message to his people, warning them what would happen if they did not obey him. The years of trouble had come. Now the prophet had kind words to say. He spoke of God's love and forgiveness.

"This is God's message to you," he wrote. "Someday I will make a new covenant with my people, not like the covenant I made with their fathers when I took them out of the land of Egypt. That covenant they broke. But I will put my law in their hearts; and I will be their God and they shall be my people. They shall all know me, from the least to the greatest. I will forgive them."

THE END OF JUDAH

But in half-empty Jerusalem King Zedekiah would not listen to Jeremiah. Judah tried to fight to get free from Babylonia. Then a huge army came from Babylonia. They smashed the thick walls of Jerusalem. They burned the Temple and every large building in the city. They took many more people to Babylon as prisoners.

The Babylonians let Jeremiah stay in Jerusalem. Before the fall of the city, Jeremiah had bought a field near Anathoth, the village where he had been born. It was his way of saying that peace would come and that God would bring his people home again someday.

But in the ruins of Jerusalem there was no peace. Some of the people fled to Egypt and forced Jeremiah to go with them. After that, nothing more was heard of this great prophet.

Judah had fallen. Its people were scattered. Beautiful Jerusalem was a heap of ashes and blackened stones. The Promised Land lay empty and wasted. Only God could help his people now.

11. Ezekiel: God's Watchman in a Faraway Land

In a land far from the walls of Jerusalem, in the city of Babylon, a new prophet began to speak for God. His name was Ezekiel, and once, long ago in his homeland, he had been a priest in the Temple. Now he was a captive in Babylon like many others whom the Babylonians had dragged away when they attacked Jerusalem the first time.

God chose Ezekiel to be his watchman in Babylon. As a watchman, Ezekiel must stand guard to see that his people remembered God. So Ezekiel the prophet spoke to remind his people never to forget the Lord God. He warned them that if they did not worship and obey God, they would displease God. It was his duty to speak for God, even when his people turned their backs and refused to listen.

Ezekiel was unlike any other prophet of the people of God, for he did strange things so that everyone would notice him

and pay attention. When Ezekiel told how God had punished his people, he clapped his hands and stamped his foot. He scratched a picture on a clay brick to show how Babylonian armies attacked Jerusalem. Many times he acted out what he wanted to say. And the prophet spoke of dreams and strange visions in which God spoke to him. In many ways the prophet made God's message so clear and real that the people could see all that God was saying, as if it were a picture painted on a wall.

SHEPHERDS OF GOD'S PEOPLE

"Listen, O leaders of Israel!" Ezekiel said as he spoke to those who had been princes and priests of Judah. "This is what

God is saying to you: 'I wanted you to be like shepherds for my people. But you were not good shepherds. You did not feed my people with my word. You did not teach them my ways. You did not heal the sick or help those who were crippled to walk. You did not look for those who had forgotten me or try to bring them back. You did not love my people. You loved only yourselves and cared only about making yourselves rich.

'Now I, the Lord God, will be the shepherd of my own sheep. I will look for them and rescue them. I will save them and bring them back to their own land. I will show them my love and teach them my ways. And they shall know that I, the Lord their God, am with them, and that they are my people!' "

THAT THE NATIONS WILL KNOW

Then Ezekiel said to the people: "This is what God is saying to you: 'I wanted you to show all nations what I am like. I wanted you to tell all nations that I am God. But you did not follow my ways. You would not listen to me. You worshiped gods that were not gods. You made the nations laugh at me!

'So I had to destroy you because you would not remember that you belong to me. I scattered you among the nations and let Assyria and Babylonia have power over you. And even now you complain and say, "God is not fair!" It is *you* who are not fair! Why do you want to die, O Israel? The Lord does not want anyone to die; turn back to me and live!

'Now I will tell you what I will do. I will take you out of this land and bring you back to your own land. I will give you a new heart and a new spirit so that you may walk in my ways and obey my commandments and live as my people. And you shall be my people, and I will be your God.

'But this you must understand: You do not deserve the good thing I will do for you. Yet I will do it so that all people of the earth may know that I am God. Then when you return to your land, the nations will know that God has done this, and they will praise my name.' "

THE VALLEY OF THE DRY BONES

And Ezekiel told the people what God had showed him in a strange dream: "In my dream God set me down in a valley," he said, "and the valley was full of dry bones. And God said to me, 'Tell these bones that I will make them live again. And they will know that I am the Lord.'

"So I did what the Lord commanded. And as I looked, behold, the bones came together, and they were covered with flesh and skin, and they breathed and lived! The valley that was full of dry bones now was full of living men!

"Now this is what the dream means: Only God can give life. Only God can give you a new life. He will make you able to know him and love him. He will bring you back to your land. And you will know that the Lord is God, and you will be his people."

So Ezekiel told the people all that God showed him. He helped them to remember that they belonged to God. This is how Ezekiel was God's watchman in faraway Babylon.

12. *Isaiah: Glad News for the Nations!*

Long years went by and still the people of Judah had to stay in the land of Babylon. Many no longer hoped that God would ever bring them back home. "The Lord has forgotten us," they said. "He will not keep his promise."

Then one day a glad, new song rang across the land:
Comfort, comfort my people,
   says your God.
Speak tenderly to Jerusalem,
   and cry to her
that her warfare is ended,
   that her sin is forgiven!

Shout with a loud voice!
Say to the cities of Judah,
   "Behold your God!"

No, the Lord had not broken his promise! He had not forgotten his people. He was getting ready to bring them home!

A LIGHT FOR THE WORLD

Who was the prophet who sang the welcome song of God's love and forgiveness to his discouraged people? No one remembers his name! Today we call him Second Isaiah, because his songs were added to the book which also has the words of another prophet named Isaiah. But it does not matter that we do not know his name; we can never forget his message.

He told the people that God was bringing them back to their land. But even more important, he told them why.

"God wants Israel to be his servant," Isaiah told the people. "God has chosen Israel to do a special thing for the world. You must be like a light to show all the people of the world that God loves them and wants them to be his people! Israel must teach the world that only God can save them and bring them back to a happy life with him. This is the reason God is bringing you back to your land."

GOD WILL SEND HIS SERVANT

God showed Isaiah the wonderful thing he would do. "I will send my *Servant,* and he will save my people and bring them back to me. They will not know him when he comes. They will not listen to him; they will laugh at him. They will hate him and hurt and kill him. But he will be willing even to die so that they can come back to the God who loves them.

IN THE TIME OF THE PROPHETS

"Then the world will know what I have done for them, and they will bow down and worship me. They will say, 'Now we know that this was God's *Servant*. Now we understand that God made us and that God saved us. We belong to God. But we were like lost sheep that strayed away from God. And God sent his *Servant* to bring us back to him. God's *Servant* suffered for us and died so that we could live! Now we know how much God loves us, because his *Servant* died to forgive our sin.'"

Who was the *Servant* God would send? The people of Israel did not know. Even Isaiah did not know. But we know—because we know Jesus!

Isaiah: Glad News for the Nations!   123

13. Nehemiah: A City Is Built Again

Like small mountain streams that trickle over rocks in a spring thaw, the people began to return to their homeland in the land of Judah. And because Judah had been their home, they were ever after called the Jews. The Babylonian kings were gone, and now the strong, new empire of Persia ruled. And from Cyrus, the great Persian king, had come good news to all the captive peoples: "You are free to go back to your own land. Build your cities again. Worship your God."

But many Jewish people chose to stay right where they were. "We were born in this land," said the young men. "We have never seen the Jerusalem our fathers talk about."

Others thought it would be too hard to go back. "Jerusalem is a ruined city of ashes and blackened stones," they said.

A few brave people did go back. They built houses again and planted the burned-out fields in the wasted land. They even built a new temple. It was very small and not nearly so fine as Solomon's temple, but once more the people could worship God in their own land.

THE KING'S CUPBEARER

In the palace of the great king of Persia there lived a Jew named Nehemiah. He was wise and intelligent, and the king had made him his cupbearer. It was Nehemiah's job to serve each cup of wine to the king and to test it to see that no enemy had poisoned it. A cupbearer was a trusted friend of the king.

One day messengers from Judah came to the palace. Nehemiah asked the man, "What is happening in Jerusalem? How are my people in the land of Judah?"

"The people of Judah are in great trouble and shame," they answered. "The walls of Jerusalem are still broken down, and its gates have been destroyed by fire. It is a ruined and deserted city. No one is even trying to rebuild it."

Nehemiah sat down and wept. He wept because he knew Jerusalem could never again be a strong capital city for the people of God if it had no walls to protect it from its enemies.

"O Lord God of Heaven," Nehemiah prayed, "you have kept your promises and showed steadfast love. Hear the prayer of your servant for all my people. I and my father's house have sinned. And we have not kept the commandments which you gave us through your servant Moses. Because we were unfaithful to you, you took us far from our land and scattered us among the nations. But you promised to bring us back to our own land so that your name and your saving power might be known to all the world. You chose us to be your servants and your people. You saved us by your great power and your strong hand. Now, O Lord, hear my prayer. Let the king allow me to return to the city of my fathers, that I may build it again."

When Nehemiah went in to the king, the king saw that his cupbearer was sad. "Why do you look so unhappy?"

Nehemiah was afraid to speak of the thoughts in his mind, for if the king were displeased, he would dismiss him in disgrace. But Nehemiah spoke up bravely. "How can I not be sad when the city of my fathers is in ruins?"

The king understood how Nehemiah felt. He let Nehemiah go back to his own land and made him governor of Judah. The king gave him a letter to the keeper of his forest: "Give Nehemiah all the timber he needs to build the gates of the city and its walls."

RISE UP AND BUILD!

When Nehemiah came to the city of Jerusalem, he found it in ruins just as the messengers had said. The people were not proud of their city. They had given up trying to build Jerusalem into a city that would show the world they were proud to be the people of God. They no longer believed that God would help them.

One night Nehemiah took a few men with him and made a secret inspection of the walls and gates. They started at the Valley Gate and saw piles of broken stone and rubble. They

126   *IN THE TIME OF THE PROPHETS*

moved on to the Jackel's Wall and to the Dung Gate; then on to where the Fountain Gate and the King's Pool used to be. The story was the same; everything was ruined. They looked at the ruined walls from the valley and then came back in.

In the morning Nehemiah gathered all the chief men of Jerusalem. "Our city lies in ruins," Nehemiah said. "All our gates are burned. Our neighbors laugh at us. We are as nothing in the eyes of all the people around us." Everyone agreed. Nehemiah went on. "Let Jerusalem rise again with strong walls on all sides. Then the people will know we have something important to defend. They will know what God has done for us. Now let us rise up and build!"

BUILDING THE WALL

Quickly Nehemiah ordered timber and stone and mortar. He called the people together and divided them into teams. Each team was to work on a certain section of the walls. The team of priests worked to rebuild the Sheep Gate. Next to them worked the men of Jericho. And so on around the whole city. Men cleared out rubbish and cut and carried stone. What a sight it was! Everywhere men were working together, building again the huge, long walls.

As soon as the news spread, enemies came. They hooted and jeered at the workmen: "Are you building a wall out of rubbish and burned stones?" they laughed. "If a fox goes up on your wall, he will break it down!" But the men kept on working.

Then they tried to make the workers afraid. Soldiers threatened to come and kill the workers. But the people prayed and set guards day and night.

And Nehemiah said to the people and their leaders, "Do not be afraid. Remember the Lord! Fight for your neighbors, for your families, and for your homes. And the Lord our God will fight for us."

Nehemiah stationed men in the spaces along the walls. Each one carried a sword and a spear or bow. During the day, half the workers worked on the walls, while the other half held their shields and weapons ready. And every worker wore his sword at his side. Workers from nearby farms and villages spent the night inside the city, so that nothing could keep them from going back to their work the next day. Each day from sunrise to sunset the people worked. When it was too dark to see, they lay down to rest; but each man kept his weapon in his hand all night!

Then Judah's enemies tried a trick. They came to Nehemiah and said, "Come and let us meet together in one of the villages and talk this over."

Nehemiah: A City Is Built Again

But Nehemiah would not go because he knew they wanted to harm him. So the enemies sent a messenger to threaten Nehemiah: "You are building the wall because you want to fight the Persian king. We will tell the Persians that you want to be king yourself!"

Nehemiah answered, "What you say is not true!" And he prayed to God to make him strong and brave and to help him keep on with the work.

On the fifty-second day the workers put the last stone in place. The walls were finished! And when the enemies of Judah heard that the walls were finished, they were afraid, for they saw that God had helped his people build their city again.

From every village of Judah people came for a great celebration to dedicate the walls to God. The princes of Judah marched in two companies along the top of the walls, one company to the right and one to the left. And the people followed, singing songs of thanks to God. At the Gate of the Guard they met and went down to the Temple. There they gave thanks to the Lord God and offered sacrifices and rejoiced.

People came back to live in Jerusalem and built new houses. And on every Sabbath the people sang hymns of praise and brought their offerings to God.

GOD'S PEOPLE REMEMBER

One day a priest named Ezra called all the people together. He stood on a wooden pulpit and opened a new book of the laws God had given to Moses.

"Only the Lord is God," Ezra told the people. "He has made heaven and earth, and everything in it. It is he who gives life and cares for it.

"He chose Abraham and made a covenant with him to give his descendants the land of Canaan. And he kept his promise.

"He saw the trouble of our fathers in the land of Egypt and brought them out of slavery. In a pillar of cloud by day and a pillar of fire by night he led them through the wilderness to the holy mountain. There he made a covenant with them; and they became his people, and he was their God. He gave them his laws and commandments.

"But our fathers were proud and stubborn, and they did not obey his commandments. They made a golden calf and worshiped it, but even then God did not leave them. He gave them bread for their hunger and water for their thirst, and he brought them into the land and made them a people.

"But our people did not obey the Lord. They worshiped gods who were no gods, and they would not listen to the prophets of God. The kings and priests did not love God or keep his laws. But still God did not leave us, for he is merciful.

"He was faithful to us, but we were wicked and sinful. Therefore he took us out of our land and scattered us. Then after years of sorrow he brought us back to be his people."

So God gave the tiny nation of Judah a new beginning. The people were at home again. And they promised to worship God and to serve him always.

Part 5

Jesus, the Promised Messiah

14. The Travelers

The Judean night was cold and still. Black shadows swallowed the olive groves. Tall cypress trees along the lonely south road to Bethlehem stood like Roman spears in the cold starlight. It was late. The town where the great King David had been born so many long years before was asleep.

At Bethlehem's gate a watchman stamped his cold feet and blew into his cupped hands to warm them. He wished the long night watch were over. He wished he were home in his warm bed.

In the lighted doorway of the inn two Roman soldiers stood talking. The watchman saw the light glint on their helmets and short swords. "Romans!" he thought bitterly. "Pah! Will we never be rid of them? Will our country never belong to us again?"

The Jews were bitter about having these outsiders in their land. Hadn't God chosen the Jews to be his own people? Hadn't he made his promises to them? It was not right, the watchman thought, that foreign rulers should tell them what to do. It was not right to pay taxes to rulers from far away.

The watchman shook his head sadly. Long ago Nehemiah and Ezra had helped their people start over again in this land. Once more the Jews had dreamed of becoming a great nation. They remembered God's promise to send his Servant to save them. They thought he would be a great king, like King David. They hoped he would come soon.

But it had not happened that way. Many years went by. Nehemiah and Ezra died, and still their land belonged to the Persian king. Then Greek rulers took their land away from the Persians. And now Palestine belonged to the mighty Romans. It was true that the Jews had their own king. But what Jew could like cruel King Herod? And even Herod had to do what the Romans told him. Otherwise, he could not be king.

"And now this tax," the watchman grumbled. "As if we were not poor enough! Our towns and farms are full of poor people. A poor man like me can hardly feed his family. And now we must give more money to the Romans."

It was true. From faraway Rome the order had come: Everyone must go to the city his family came from. There his name must be registered in a book to pay taxes to the Roman emperor. Like every town in Palestine, Bethlehem was still full of such travelers.

"Well, someday it will all be different," the watchman thought. "Someday God will send his Messiah to save us, just as he promised. The Messiah will make our land peaceful and rich. He will help the poor people of Palestine."

The watchman's mind was full of thoughts about the Messiah. He paid no attention to the man leading a donkey toward the gate. He hardly noticed the woman on the donkey's back or the sleeping child cradled in her arms. Even before they had started down the road away from Bethlehem, he had forgotten them. They were just poor Jews, who had registered for the tax and were going home again.

He did not know that this baby was the Messiah. He did not know that God was keeping his promise!

IN THE HILLS

In the hills south of Bethlehem a small band of young men huddled around a fire in the mouth of a cave. They were called Zealots. They hated the Romans who ruled their country. They looked for ways to harm them.

They, too, were waiting for the Messiah.

"Someday he will come," one of the Zealots was saying. "You'll see. God will not let our country be ruled forever by these Romans." He spat into the fire, as if the word had a bad taste.

"But when? When will he come?" asked another man, who was polishing his sword. "We have waited so long! Sometimes I think it will never happen."

JESUS, THE PROMISED MESSIAH

The first man leaned forward, his eyes blazing like coals. "He will come," he said softly. "Remember God's promise. Soon—very soon—he will send his Messiah to lead us. What a day that will be! All of Israel will be his army. We will drive the Romans out of our land. Israel will be great and free again!"

"How will we know him?" a boy asked eagerly. "Are you sure we will know who he is?"

"Know him!" the first man laughed. He clapped the boy on the shoulder. "Of course we'll know him, lad! How could we not know a great warrior king like the Messiah!"

"Listen! What's that?" The Zealot band grew suddenly quiet—listening. From the road below came the soft clopping of a donkey's hooves. One of the men sprang to the rocks to find out what was happening.

In a minute he was back. "Just some poor travelers. A man, a woman on a donkey, a baby. Nobody important."

The men went back to their talk and their dreams. Not one guessed that the Messiah was passing by.

ON THE ROAD

It was a long way from Bethlehem to Egypt. But every step of the swaying donkey brought the travelers closer to safety. For God had warned Joseph in a dream, "King Herod will try to kill the child."

Mary and Joseph had not waited for morning to come. In the darkness they had bundled together their few belongings. They had wrapped the baby Jesus warmly, and they had left

Bethlehem by night. They had to take the baby into Egypt and live there until it was safe to come back.

It was all so strange, Mary thought. Her baby was the Son of God! This tiny little boy who slept in her arms was God's own Son. How could it be? What did it mean? She did not know, but she was sure it was so.

She remembered the shepherds who had come to see the child in the cattle stall in Bethlehem. What a strange story they told—of an angel who had come to them in the fields where they were tending their sheep. And the angel said to them:

Be not afraid; for behold, I bring you
good news of a great joy which will come
to all the people; for to you is born
this day in the city of David a Savior,
who is Christ the Lord.

The Travelers

"A Savior," Mary murmured, looking down at the sleeping Jesus. "A Savior, who is Christ the Lord."

She remembered the wise men from the East. For weeks they had followed a strange star. And the star had led them to Bethlehem, to the very place where Jesus was! Mary remembered the love and joy that lighted the dark, tired faces when they saw the child. She remembered how they had knelt down before the baby—as if he were a king. As if he were God himself!

And she remembered the old man in the Temple. He had taken the baby in his arms. Tears had streamed down his wrinkled face. "Lord, now let thy servant depart in peace," he had said, "for my eyes have seen thy salvation!" It was as if he could see God in the baby Jesus!

"But he looks like any other baby," Mary thought. "How could they know?"

The baby stirred and cried out in his sleep. "Hush, little son," Mary crooned. "You are safe. God will keep you safe. Someday we will go back home to Nazareth. You will run and play in sunny Galilee. You will grow tall and strong. And I will teach you about your Father."

The swaying donkey moved on through the night.

What did it all mean? Mary wondered. What wonderful thing was God planning to do for the world through Jesus?

JESUS, THE PROMISED MESSIAH

15. A Voice in the Wilderness

What was happening at the Jordan River? From all over Judea people were coming—

rich people and poor people,
old men and young boys,
Roman soldiers and Jewish Zealots,
tax collectors, fishermen, farmers, shepherds,
teachers and lawyers, priests and scribes!

They came from nearby and far away. They came from the big city of Jerusalem and from the little town of Bethlehem. Some even came from fishermen's huts along the Sea of Galilee.

Every day there were more people who came to see the man at the River Jordan. Who was he? What was he doing? Why was everybody so excited about him?

His name was John. He was a strange-looking man. His coat was made of rough camel's hair. A leather belt was knotted around his waist. He ate the food of the wilderness—berries and locusts and wild honey. His feet were bare. His skin was brown from the wilderness sun and rough from the wind.

"He looks like Elijah," people whispered to one another. Hundreds of years before, a rough-clad prophet named Elijah had spoken for God to the people of Israel. The Jews had heard their fathers say, "Someday Elijah will come back." They wondered if John were really Elijah.

John was a big man with a big voice. And what he said was big and important, too.

"Repent!" he shouted. "Change your ways before it is too late. The kingdom of heaven is near!"

"The kingdom of heaven!" people said to one another. "What does he mean?"

"He must mean the Messiah is coming!" some said.

"Maybe *he* is the Messiah himself!" others guessed.

Whatever he meant, John made it sound like the most important message in the world. "You must listen!" he cried. "Now is the time to tell God you are sorry and ask him to forgive you." He reminded the people of the covenant God had made with them. He reminded them that they were the people of God. "You must live like people of God," he said.

This was what all the prophets had told the people. This was what Elijah had said, and Amos, and Jeremiah. John sounded just like the prophets of long ago. But he was different, too.

He told the people they must do something to show that their hearts were changed. They must be baptized.

Day after day the people came. Many believed what John said. They were sorry for their sins. They wanted to turn back to God's ways. And John baptized them in the River Jordan.

"What else must we do?" they asked John.

"If you have two coats," John told them, "share with your neighbor who does not have one. Share your food with those who are hungry."

To the tax collectors he said, "Do not take more money than people owe you."

"Do not rob anyone," he told the soldiers. "Do not lie about anyone."

Some people did not like what John said. They did not want him to say they were doing bad things. They were angry when he told them they were not living as God's people. They would not believe that the kingdom of heaven was so near.

WHO ARE YOU?

In Jerusalem, the Temple leaders began to worry. "Who is that man out there in the desert, making a hero of himself?" they wondered. They sent priests and teachers to find out.

"Who are you?" they asked John.

"I am not the Messiah," John answered.

"Then who are you?" they asked. "Are you Elijah?"

"No, I am not," he said.

JESUS, THE PROMISED MESSIAH

"Well then, tell us who you are!" they said. "We must have an answer for those who sent us."

John said, "I am the voice crying in the wilderness: *Prepare the way of the Lord!*"

The priests and teachers looked at each other. They had heard these words before! Long ago Isaiah had promised that God would send a messenger. The messenger would help the people get ready for the Messiah. Isaiah had said, "He will be a voice in the wilderness." Now John was saying that he was the messenger!

"But if you are not the Messiah and not Elijah, why do you baptize the people?" the priests wanted to know.

"I baptize with water," John told them. "But someone is coming who is more powerful than I. I do not even deserve to untie the strings of his sandals. When he comes, he will baptize you with the Holy Spirit of God."

The priests and teachers were frightened. They did not understand. What was this man talking about, they wondered. Was he really God's messenger? Was it really time now to get ready to meet the Messiah?

THE SPECIAL BAPTISM

"Repent! Be baptized!" John's big voice rang out. "Show that you want to live God's way. Soon God's kingdom will be right here with you."

It was a day like other days. Many people stood listening to John. Many were coming down to the river to be baptized.

Suddenly it seemed to John that the world had turned upside down. He stared at the strong young man waiting to be baptized. The man was from Galilee. He was a carpenter from the village of Nazareth. His name was Jesus.

"You!" John said softly. "How can I baptize you? No, you must baptize me!"

But Jesus smiled. "This is what I want," he said. "This is what God wants."

So Jesus knelt in the shallow water, just as other people had done who were looking for God's forgiveness. And John baptized him.

Later John told about the wonderful thing that happened when he baptized Jesus. "I heard a voice from heaven say, *'This is my beloved Son.'* And the Spirit of God came down on Jesus like a dove."

It was a special sign that God lived in Jesus.

16. Finding God's Way

Jesus knew that now it was time to do the work God had sent him to do. But how should he begin? What did God want him to do?

Jesus went away to a lonely place in the wilderness, all by himself. There he prayed that God show him what to do.

Long days and nights went by, and still the answer did not come. Jesus felt hungry. In the wilderness there was very little a person could eat. There were only dry twigs and stones.

"If you are really the Son of God, turn these stones into bread."

The thought came so quickly it surprised Jesus! Turn the stones into bread! Was that God's answer? "Why should the Son of God ever have to be hungry?" Jesus thought. Why should anyone be hungry? Yes, he could give the people what they wanted. He could do wonderful miracles, and this would prove he was the Messiah.

But was this what God wanted? Was God sending him to feed the hungry people of Palestine? Many people thought the most important thing God could do for them was to give them enough to eat.

"But that is not the most important thing," Jesus thought. He remembered a verse from Scripture: "*Man shall not live by bread alone.*" "No," Jesus thought. "People do need bread, but God has something much more important than bread to give the people."

Then another thought came to Jesus. "If you are the Son of God, prove it by throwing yourself from the top of the Temple. Hasn't God promised that his angels will protect you? Isn't that what the Scriptures say?"

He could get plenty of attention that way, all right. But Jesus knew that these ideas did not come from God. They were evil ideas! The Devil was trying to make him do what God did not want him to do.

"The Scriptures do say God will protect me," Jesus said aloud. "But the Scriptures also say, '*You shall not test God.*'" Jesus was sure that God would care for him. He did not need to throw himself off the Temple roof to prove it.

But the Devil had still another idea for Jesus. "The Jews are waiting for a ruler," he whispered. "All the people will fight in your army. Then you can drive the Roman enemy out of the country. And everyone will gladly obey you."

"No!" Jesus pushed the idea aside. "This is not what God wants," he thought. "If I try to be that kind of king, I will be serving the Devil instead of God!"

So he said, "Get away from me, Satan! The Scriptures say, '*You shall worship the Lord your God, and him only shall you serve.*'"

The long struggle was over for now. Jesus was tired. But he was ready now to begin his Father's work because he knew what he must do. He must show people what God was like. He must show them how much God loved them.

Jesus knew that there would be many who would not listen to him. Some would laugh at him. Others would be angry and afraid. They would try to hurt him and even kill him.

It would not be easy to be God's Servant Messiah. But it was the only way to bring a sinful people back to God.

Part 6

Jesus, Friend and Helper

17. Come and See

The Sea of Galilee threw back the light of the morning sun like a mirror. Fishermen had tugged their boats ashore. They had sold the day's catch in nearby Capernaum and Bethsaida. Now they were stringing up nets to dry and mending torn places.

Simon the fisherman was worried. His big hands moved skillfully over his net, but his thoughts were far away. He was worried about his brother. Where was Andrew, he wondered. Days had gone by since he went away to hear John the Baptist. He should be back by now!

Simon's back was burned brown. The soles of his feet were toughened by the hot sand. He did not mind. He loved the sea. When he and Andrew were little boys, they had gone out in the boats with their father. They could not imagine a better life than a fisherman's.

"Where is your brother today?" a fisherman called to Simon.

"Listening to the preacher in the wilderness, I guess," Simon called back. "Andrew can't stay away from him."

Simon finished folding his net. He settled down in his boat to rest. What was keeping Andrew, he worried. Something must have happened!

Simon knew that important men in Jerusalem did not like John the Baptist. One of these days there would surely be trouble. But Andrew and Simon were not easily frightened. They had gone out to sea on nights when other fishermen did not dare to go. They had fought their way out of many troubles before. But they had always been together. Did Andrew need help now, Simon wondered.

Suddenly his worries were gone. There was Andrew, running down the beach, shouting Simon's name.

"We have found the Messiah!" Andrew shouted, as he jumped into the boat, rocking it wildly.

Simon grabbed the sides of the boat to steady himself. "The Messiah!" he said. "Andrew, what are you talking about? Where have you been?"

"With the Messiah!" Andrew threw his arms around Simon's big shoulders in a giant hug. "That's what I'm trying to tell you. He's here. He's right here in Bethsaida!"

"You mean John the Baptist?" Simon said. "But I thought—"

Andrew did not wait for Simon to finish. "Not John,"

he said. "Don't you remember how John always said he was getting people ready for another person?"

"Yes," said Simon, "but what other person?"

"Jesus of Nazareth," Andrew answered.

"Jesus of Nazareth?" Simon was puzzled. "What makes you think he is the Messiah? And why were you with him, anyway? I thought you went to hear John!"

Andrew laughed. "One question at a time! We did go to hear John. But while we were with him, this Jesus came by. And John said to us, 'This is the Son of God. Listen to him!' "

"The Son of God!" Simon exclaimed.

"So we followed him," Andrew went on. "We wanted to know more about him. We wanted to know whether everything John said was true."

"What happened?" Simon asked.

"When Jesus saw us following him, he asked, 'Why are you following me? What do you want?' We asked him where he was staying, and he said, 'Come and see.' So we did! We have been with him all day, and—oh, Simon, you must come and see for yourself!"

The next day fishermen sailed out on the Sea of Galilee as usual. But one boat was tied to its stake. It swung lazily back and forth in the breeze-blown sea. The dry net lay folded where Simon had tucked it away the day before.

Andrew and Simon had found the Messiah. They had left their home on the Sea of Galilee to follow him.

Along the shore two other brothers were mending their nets. They were James and John, sons of old Zebedee the fisherman.

How often James and John had talked of the day when God would send the Messiah! At night in their boats on the Sea of Galilee they would talk over all that John the Baptist had said. "Who is the one who is coming?" they would ask each other. In the morning as they mended their nets they would say to each other, "Will we know him when he comes?"

And then one day he was there. For a long time Jesus stood looking at the two brothers. It was as if he could see in their faces that they were searching for him.

Then he said, "Follow me!"

James and John looked at each other. This was the man Simon and Andrew had left everything to follow. James and John put down their nets. They said goodbye to their father and went with Jesus.

UNDER A FIG TREE

Nathanael rested his back against a fig tree and thought about the promised Messiah. He watched the sun through half-closed eyes. "I wonder what he will be like," he thought. "Will he come out of the sky like a great warrior king?" Nathanael tried to imagine how that would be. Maybe the sky would open up. Light would pour down like a great road. Then the Messiah would come, his sword in his hand.

Suddenly a hand was shaking Nathanael's shoulder. "Nathanael!" a voice was saying. Nathanael jerked himself out of his daydreams. His friend Philip was leaning over him, his eyes shining with excitement.

"We have found him!" he was saying. "We have found the one the prophets told us would come!"

"What!" Nathanael was wide awake now. "Who is he?"

"Jesus of Nazareth!" Philip replied.

Nathanael shook his head and settled back against the fig tree. He knew the village of Nazareth. He had seen the poor, dirty streets and the little houses. Nazareth was not even on an important road. Philip must be wrong. Nazareth could never be famous for anything!

"Can anything good come out of Nazareth?" he said.

Philip grabbed his friend's hand and pulled him to his feet. "Come and see," he answered.

When Jesus saw Nathanael coming toward him, he said, "Here comes an honest Israelite!"

Nathanael was amazed. "How do you know me?"

"I saw you under the fig tree before Philip called you," Jesus said.

Nathanael stared at Jesus. "Teacher, you are the Son of God! You are really the King of Israel!"

Jesus laughed, "Do you believe it just because I said I saw you under the fig tree?" he asked. He put his hand on Nathanael's shoulder. "You shall see greater things than these," he promised.

Come and See

So Jesus went to the towns and villages of Galilee and chose twelve men to be his special followers.

There were *Simon,* whom Jesus called Peter, and his brother *Andrew.*

Then came two other fishermen brothers, *James* and *John.*

There were *Philip* and his friend *Nathanael,* who was sometimes called Bartholomew.

One was a tax collector named *Matthew,* and one was a Zealot named *Simon.*

Finally there were *Thomas* and a second *James, Thaddeus,* and *Judas Iscariot.*

These twelve men went with Jesus wherever he went. He began to teach them about his Father. Jesus wanted to get them ready to tell others about God's love.

"It will not be easy," he told them. "You must give up everything to follow me. You must leave your families and your homes and your work. You will never be rich or important. There will be danger. But God will be with you."

The twelve disciples listened eagerly. They were not sure just what Jesus had come to do. They did not see how they could help him. "We are not good speakers," they thought. "We are not important persons. Many other people know Scripture better than we do."

But Jesus wanted them—that was what mattered. They believed that Jesus had been sent by God. And they were willing to give their lives to him.

They had come and seen. They were ready to follow.

JESUS, FRIEND AND HELPER

18. With Jesus in Capernaum

Jesus walked along the road to Capernaum with his disciples.

Simon Peter knew this town well for he had lived here in a fisherman's hut near the shore of the lake. Capernaum had been his home before he had left everything to follow Jesus. Peter's wife and her mother still lived here. But Peter had been away for many weeks.

Capernaum was a busy town. Traders from Damascus traveled through this town on their way to Jerusalem. Roman soldiers were stationed here to guard the country and to see that the Roman laws were kept. Poor farmers labored under the hot sun for rich landowners. Potters and tanners, carpenters and weavers worked at their trades in the crowded market-place. The stone docks at the edge of the Sea of Galilee were always crowded with men mending nets and packing fish in barrels of salt.

Capernaum was a town where rich merchants and land-owners lived. But it was also a city of the poor. The narrow streets reeked with the smells of rotting fruit and fish. Swarms of flies and insects bit and stung and brought disease. Sickness and hunger were everywhere. Cripples sat at the gates of the city begging for small gifts of money. Men with a terrible disease that ate their flesh and bones waited outside the gates. They were called lepers. They were hungry for kindness and help. But no one tried to help the lepers. "They are unclean," people said.

Capernaum was a town that needed help and healing.

A MAN WHO TRUSTED JESUS

As Jesus and his disciples came into Capernaum they were surprised to see a Roman centurion hurrying toward them. Had they broken some law, the disciples wondered. Was there going to be trouble?

The centurion was gentle and polite. "Sir," he said, "my servant is very ill. He cannot move, and he is in terrible pain." The centurion wanted Jesus to help him.

The disciples looked at one another in surprise. Would Jesus help a Roman?

Jesus did not need time to decide what he would do. "I will come and heal him," he said.

The centurion answered, "Sir, I am not good enough for you to come into my house. Only say the word and I know my servant will be healed."

JESUS, FRIEND AND HELPER

Now the disciples were truly amazed. They knew that a hundred soldiers did whatever this centurion commanded. If he said, "Go," they went. If he said, "Come," they came. He was an important man. Now he was saying that he was not good enough to have Jesus in his house!

Jesus also was astonished. "I have not found anyone in Israel with such great faith," he said to his disciples.

Then he turned to the centurion. "Go. It will be exactly as you have believed."

And at that very moment the centurion's servant became well.

AT THE SYNAGOGUE

It was the Sabbath, and Jesus and his disciples went to the synagogue. The news had spread that Jesus was a teacher who knew the Scriptures well. And so it happened that Jesus was asked to read and explain the Scriptures.

The people of Capernaum listened to the stranger. Soon they began to nudge one another and whisper among themselves. Who was this man? How did he know the Scriptures so well?

"This man is not like our teachers," said a merchant to his friend. "He speaks as if God himself had told him what to say."

An old man sitting near the front of the room smiled as he listened. "He is talking to me," the old man whispered to himself.

"Is it possible that what he is saying is true?" a farmer wondered. "Does God really care about a poor man like me?"

The scribes began comparing what Jesus taught with what they taught. They knew it was not the same. "The laws do not seem important to him," they thought. "How could anyone get into heaven through something that happens in his heart?" The scribes looked worried.

They leaned over to whisper to one another, "We are in for trouble. See how the people are listening to everything he is saying. We should never have let him speak."

Some of the elders were angry. "What he says cannot be true. He is a false prophet," they decided.

At first no one noticed a wild-looking man who rushed from the back of the synagogue, waving his arms frantically. His beard was tangled and uncombed. His eyes gleamed with a wild excitement. Suddenly there he stood in the middle of the room.

"What have you to do with us, Jesus of Nazareth?" he shouted. "Have you come to destroy us? I know who you are— the Holy One of God!"

The young men of the congregation leaped up to take the man away. "He is out of his mind!" the older men exclaimed. "Evil spirits rule him; devils live inside him. Take him outside!"

The man's body shook with fear. He kept screaming that Jesus was the Holy One of God.

"Be quiet and come out of him!" Jesus ordered.

JESUS, FRIEND AND HELPER

There, in the hushed silence of the synagogue, the man became calm. His arms fell quietly to his side. His body stopped twitching and shaking. The fear left his eyes. His terrible illness was over.

"What is this?" the astonished people of Capernaum asked.

"What new teaching is this? He commands even the evil spirits, and they obey him!" they marveled.

People hurried away to tell friends and neighbors about the strange and wonderful things they had seen and heard. They would never forget what had happened in their synagogue that day.

AT SIMON'S HOUSE

When Jesus and his disciples left the synagogue, Simon ran ahead of the others. His wife's mother was sick with a terrible fever. Simon had asked Jesus to come to see her.

At the doorway of the little clay-brick house, Simon's wife was waiting. On other Sabbaths she had gone to the synagogue with the women. Today she had stayed home to care for her mother. Over and over she had dipped cloths in cool water. Gently she had wrapped them about her mother's tired, hot body. She had mixed herbs just as a wise old woman had told her. Some she laid on her mother's head and neck. Others she cooked to make a healing soup. But nothing helped. The fever would not leave.

Simon Peter knew as soon as he saw his wife that her

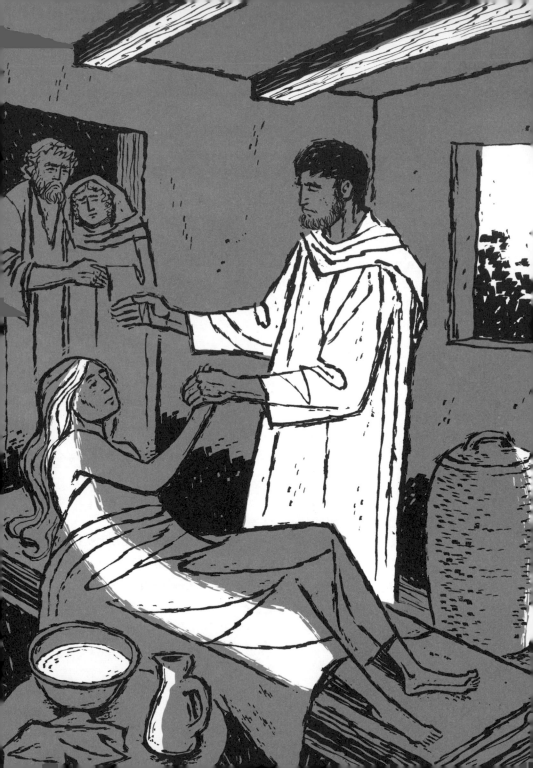

mother was no better. Before he could ask any questions, she shook her head sadly.

"There is nothing anyone can do," she said. "I have tried everything."

"Jesus is coming," Peter said to her. "He will help. You'll see."

When Andrew arrived with Jesus, Peter took Jesus inside the dark room where his wife's mother lay.

"We can do nothing," Peter's wife told Jesus. "She has eaten no food for days. She will die."

Jesus stooped down beside the old woman's sleeping mat. Gently he took her hot hand in his own. And at once the fever left her!

Peter's home was filled with joy. His wife's mother got up and cooked a meal for Jesus and the disciples. Every step she took, everything she did, every bit of food she offered her guests was like a song of thanksgiving. How near God seemed!

The news spread through the town of Capernaum that Jesus was staying in the home of Simon and Andrew.

That evening at sundown it seemed as if everyone in the whole city were outside Simon's little house! Fathers and mothers carried children whose faces were hot with fever. Cripples hobbled on canes and sticks to get near the man from Nazareth. Long, long into the dark hours of the night Jesus talked with those who had come to him for help. He touched them and healed them and sent them home to begin new lives with their families.

When at last they had all gone home, Jesus rested. But before the first light of dawn touched the hills around Capernaum, Jesus got up and went out to a lonely place to pray.

There his disciples found him when it was morning. They told him that the street had filled with people once more. "Everyone is searching for you," Simon Peter said.

JESUS, FRIEND AND HELPER

"Let us go on to the next town," Jesus answered. "I must preach the good news of the kingdom in other places also, for that is why I came."

And so the disciples followed Jesus across the hills and down into the valleys. They walked among the villages and towns of Galilee, bringing to all who would listen the love of God.

With Jesus in Capernaum

19. *Miracle on the Hillside*

The children of Bethsaida looked forward to Jesus' visits to their town. They loved to talk with him and ask him questions.

"God is very great and holy," Jesus told them. "But God is also kind and good, like the best father you can imagine." He told them that God loved them always, even when they did things that were not what he wanted. He said that if they were sorry for the wrong things they did, God would forgive them and help them to be better. He showed them ways they could thank God for loving them so much.

"If God is like Jesus," the children thought, "he is very, very wonderful."

Jesus was never too busy or too tired to be their friend. He always seemed to know just how they felt. He listened to them when they had something happy to share or when they felt sad and lonely. Sometimes he played games with them. And sometimes in the evening he would sing with them until their mothers called them to bed.

Jesus had not come to Bethsaida for many weeks. Every morning the children would run to the lake to see if a crowd were gathering on a hill or down by the fishing boats. That would mean that Jesus was probably there.

One morning before the sun had dried the spangles from the spiders' webs, a little girl jumped from her sleeping mat and ran down to the beach. She wanted to be the very first to look for Jesus. Shading her eyes from the light, she looked as hard and as long as she could. Then she sat down and watched some of the fishermen casting their nets for fish in the shallow water.

"Meta!" she heard Bart calling her. "Have you seen him?"

"No, Bart," she called back. "I was going to come and tell you, but I sat down to watch the fishermen and—"

Bart had climbed to the top of a pile of logs while Meta was talking. "Look, Meta," he shrieked. "Look! There's a boat coming from Capernaum. That's Simon and Andrew's boat. I'd know it anywhere!"

It was true. Simon and Andrew were sailing straight for Bethsaida!

"Let's tell everyone that Jesus is coming!" Meta said. "Your sister wants to take her baby to him. And old Lena wants to go, and the silversmith, and the woman who sells fruit. Hurry up, Bart. Let's tell everybody."

Bart and Meta raced each other to the well where their mothers were getting the day's water.

"Jesus is coming," they panted. "We saw his boat."

"May we go?" Meta begged her mother. "We promise not to get into any trouble—or bother anyone."

"And first we want to tell everybody that Jesus will soon be here," Bart added.

"We'll make our own lunches," Meta offered.

The two mothers nodded and smiled. "You may go," they agreed. "But be sure to come back before dark. And no quarreling!"

Meta and Bart paraded up and down the streets chanting their news:

"Jesus is coming. He's on his way.

It's going to be a wonderful day!"

Soon Meta and Bart found their friends and made their plans.

"My mother has finished her baking already," Dan boasted. "I'm sure I can bring some rolls."

"We have barley loaves, baked only yesterday," said Bart.

"And we have some baked fish I can bring along," said Meta.

"I could bring some dates," little Nat offered, "if you'll let me come along."

"Of course, we'll let you come along," Meta said, hugging Bart's little brother. "Now, let's go home and get whatever food we can find."

JESUS, FRIEND AND HELPER

The children ran to tell their parents. In a short time they were back and ready to leave. Dan brought a blanket to spread over the grass. And Tora brought raisin cookies just out of her mother's oven.

Andrew's boat was pulled up on the shore, and Jesus had gone ahead to a pleasant field on a hillside. Already people were coming to talk to him. The children greeted Jesus and sat down to watch under a shady olive tree. The girls spread out the blanket. The boys tucked the food in a low branch where the sun would not dry it out.

All morning people kept coming, not just from little Bethsaida, but from villages all over the countryside. They wanted to hear Jesus tell them about the kingdom of heaven. Many came to be healed. Others told Jesus about their troubles and begged him to tell them what they ought to do. Mothers carried little children to him and asked him to lay his hand on their heads.

By noon the children were hungry. They noticed that families were eating their lunches.

"I certainly could eat a raisin cookie," Bart said, looking at the food basket with hungry eyes.

"And the dates would taste delicious," Tora said.

"Maybe we ought to eat some of the bread and fish first," Meta said, sounding much more like a mother than a little girl.

Bart took the basket of food down and the children ate and ate, but they had brought too much.

"Put the rest back up in the tree," Tora suggested. "We may get hungry later."

After some tree swinging and tag and a few games of pebble-toss, the children were ready to settle down for the afternoon. Soon Jesus began to speak. People sat everywhere on the hillside. Thousands wanted to hear and see Jesus, and they had followed him to this place. Now everyone became quiet. The smallest children had fallen asleep. Little Nat curled up on the edge of the blanket with his head in Meta's lap. Below the field tiny waves splashed quietly against the boats.

Meta and Bart listened to Jesus. "Do not be so worried about what you are going to eat or what you are going to wear," he told the people. "Look at the birds of the air. They do not sow and reap and gather food into barns. But your Heavenly Father feeds them.

"And why are you so worried about clothing?" Jesus asked. "Look at the lilies in the fields." He pointed to bright orange flowers on the hillside. "Even King Solomon's clothes did not look finer! If God does this for flowers and grass, don't you suppose he will care even more for you?

"Your Heavenly Father knows what you need," he said. "The most important thing to look for is God's kingdom. First learn what God wants for you, and he will give you all that you need."

The hours passed quickly. Children woke from their naps. But no one moved from the hillside. It was as if no one remembered time. What if chores waited to be done at home? What if the children had to be fed? What if the fishing boats should sail out for the evening catch? No one thought of such things. Even the children forgot to watch the sun move across the sky. No one thought of going home—no one except the disciples.

Simon Peter called Andrew and Philip aside. The children heard Simon talk softly.

"It is getting late," Simon Peter said, "and these people are going to be hungry. I don't see how we can feed them."

"Some of them have been here since early morning," Andrew said.

"And those who had lunches have already eaten them," added Philip.

By this time the children were listening to the men instead of to Jesus.

"They are looking for food," Bart told the others.

"Do you think we should give them ours?" Meta asked quietly.

Nat woke up. "I'm hungry," he said.

"So is Jesus," Meta told him. "But how much food do we have left?" she asked Dan.

Dan took the basket out of the tree. The raisin cookies were all gone. The dates had been eaten and most of the fish.

"Well," said Bart, "five barley loaves and two fish aren't much to give, but we could offer them to Jesus if it would help."

Bart went up to Andrew. "We don't have much, sir," he said politely, "but we would like to give it to Jesus."

Andrew smiled at the boy and thanked him. "Of course, lad," he said. "We'll tell the Master."

The disciples knew that Bart's little bit of food would not go far. They went to Jesus and said, "This is a lonely place, and it is getting late. Perhaps you should send the people home so that they can get something to eat."

But Jesus said, "Give them something to eat."

"We do not have enough money to buy food for all these people," Philip said.

"How much food do you have?" asked Jesus.

"There is a lad here with five barley loaves and two fish," Andrew told him. "But what is that among so many people?" he added.

"Bring them to me," Jesus said.

Quickly Bart brought the little basket of food. "It's all we have left," he explained, thinking of all the raisin cookies he had eaten.

Jesus took it and thanked him. "It will be enough," he said.

Then Jesus took the loaves and the fish and gave thanks. As he prayed, he broke the loaves and divided the fish and gave them to the disciples to give to the people.

And it was as he had said. There was enough. Everyone ate and was satisfied. And after all had eaten, the disciples gathered up what was left and filled twelve baskets!

Everyone was amazed. "This is truly the One whom God promised to send us!" they said to one another. Jesus saw that they wanted to make him their king. He did not want that. Quietly he slipped away to the hills by himself.

It was getting dark. Bart and Meta folded the blanket and ran back home. It had been a wonderful day. And they had exciting news to tell!

Part 7

Jesus, a Disturbing Teacher

20. The Teacher from Nazareth

Ben walked across the marketplace to sit with the men and hear the news of the day. "They're talking about Jesus again," he thought, as he listened to the men. "Everyone is talking about the teacher from Nazareth."

"Some say he's the Messiah!" a young man was saying.

"Have you ever heard him teach?" a young lawyer asked. "I've heard other teachers explain the Scriptures. But no one else teaches like this Jesus. He makes people think about God in a new way."

Ben had heard Jesus teach, too. He remembered the day he had sat on a hillside, listening to Jesus. He could still remember Jesus saying:

"You have heard that it was said, 'You shall love your neighbor and hate your enemy.' But I say to you, Love your enemies and pray for those who persecute you."

"Love your enemies?" Ben thought. "That's hard. Does God really want us to love bad people who hurt us?"

Now the lawyer was speaking again. "Jesus often talks about the kingdom of God," he said to the other men. "He shows so plainly why the kingdom is more important than anything else in the world. When I hear him, the kingdom seems very near."

Ben agreed. He too had heard Jesus talk about the kingdom as if it were coming tomorrow. Ben remembered a story Jesus told about the hidden treasure. Jesus' words were like burrs that sometimes stick to a person's clothes. They had a way of sticking in a person's mind.

Before Ben realized what he was doing, he was telling the story of the hidden treasure to the other men. Jesus had said:

"The kingdom of heaven is like a treasure hidden in a field, which a man found and covered up; then in his joy he goes and sells all that he has and buys that field."

Then everyone had a question to ask.

"What did Jesus mean?" one old man muttered.

"What does he want us to do?" another asked. "Does he want us to sell everything we have and own nothing if we want to follow him?"

Then one of the Pharisees asked, "Why do you listen to Jesus at all? He eats with tax collectors and other wicked people."

The men were quiet for a moment. The man who had spoken was one of the most religious men in the village.

"Are you sure Jesus really sits at the same table with tax collectors?" the lawyer from Capernaum asked.

"The other night he ate at Matthew's house," the Pharisee said. "You know Matthew the tax collector. Matthew had a houseful of friends there, too. Jesus didn't seem to mind at all."

"Are you sure?" the lawyer asked again.

"Of course I'm sure," the Pharisee said. "I even asked Jesus' disciples why he ate with sinners."

"You got an answer, too," one of the men said. "Jesus himself told you:

'Those who are well have no need of a physician, but those who are sick; I came not to call the righteous, but sinners.' "

The Pharisee scowled at the men and walked away. He did not like to be reminded of what Jesus had said to him. One by one the other men quietly left the busy marketplace.

On the way home Ben kept thinking about the words of Jesus. "Jesus said that he was not sent to healthy people, but to those who are sick. What did he mean?"

21. *When Jesus Answered Questions*

Almost every time people crowded around Jesus someone had a question to ask. They asked about God. They asked about John the Baptist. They asked about the laws of God.

There seemed to be no end to questions about the laws of God. To the Jews the laws of God were very important. These were the Ten Commandments and the other laws given through Moses. People had all kinds of questions about how to keep the Commandments perfectly. The Pharisees and the scribes spent most of their time trying to understand everything about the laws of God.

When Jesus taught, he had to answer all sorts of questions. Some questions were friendly. Some were unfriendly. Enemies of Jesus asked questions to try to make him look foolish. But they could never succeed.

One day a man in the crowd wanted to ask Jesus a question. This man was an expert in the laws of Moses. He knew every law in the Scriptures. He knew the teachings of the Pharisees, who had made many new laws to explain the old laws of Moses. He had gone to school in the Temple, but Jesus had not. Probably he thought, "I can make this carpenter from Nazareth look very foolish."

The expert waited for his chance to ask a question. "Master, what must I do to be sure of eternal life?" he said.

Jesus looked straight at the man. "What does the Law tell you? What have you learned?"

The man answered, "The Law says, 'You shalt love the Lord your God with all your heart and with all your soul and with all your strength and with all your mind—and your neighbor as yourself.'"

"That is absolutely right," Jesus said. "If you will do that, you will have eternal life."

The man kept on asking questions. "But who is my neighbor?" he asked. Perhaps he thought, "That's a tough question. This fellow can't answer that one."

It was not easy to say who was a "neighbor." To a Jew, a neighbor was another Jew like himself—but not a Roman or an Egyptian or a Samaritan. A Jew would not have anything to do with "sinners." He thought that God wanted him to love only good people, that is, good Jews who did everything the Law commanded.

Jesus knew what the man was thinking. This time he decided to tell a story. In the story the man and everyone else who listened could find the answer by themselves.

Jesus told a story about a man who was traveling on the road that wound down through the wilderness hills from Jerusalem to Jericho. This road was dangerous because it passed through wild and lonely country. There were no towns and villages, no farmers' fields and orchards along the way. But robbers and bandits lived in nearby caves.

Along the way robbers jumped out on the traveler from behind a big rock and dragged him from the path. They beat him with clubs until he was unconscious. They took everything he had and even pulled off his clothes. Then they ran away and left him lying on the ground.

Other people came along the same path. The first to come was a priest. According to Jewish law a person would make himself unclean if he touched a dead person. Perhaps that is why the priest did not go near the man lying on the ground. The

JESUS, A DISTURBING TEACHER

priest thought, "No one will see me. I'll pretend I didn't see the man. Maybe he is dead and can't be helped." So the priest hurried on. He passed by on the far side of the road.

The second person to come around the bend in the road was a Levite. A Levite was a man who helped take care of the Temple in Jerusalem. He knew all about the worship of God in the Temple. The Levite saw the man, but he did not stop. Like the priest, he hurried on until he was out of sight.

Then a third person came down the path with his donkey. He was not a holy person like the priest or the Levite. He was not even a Jew, but a Samaritan. If the Jews hated anyone, it was the Samaritans. Jews disliked the Samaritans so much that they even avoided traveling through Samaria whenever they possibly could. They usually went the long way around Samaria instead.

The Samaritan stopped. He bent over the man lying on the ground and saw that he was breathing. He cleaned the man's wounds and bandaged them. He put oil on his skin to make it soft and poured wine on the cuts to disinfect them. Then he helped him on his donkey and took him to an inn. He stayed overnight with the man and took care of him. The man was too sick to travel, so the Samaritan paid the innkeeper to take care of him.

The Samaritan gave the innkeeper two silver coins and said, "Look after this man. I will come back when I return to Jerusalem. Then I will pay whatever more you spend for him."

The story was finished. Everyone had listened to find out what happened. Then Jesus turned to the man who had been asking questions.

"Which of the three men was a *neighbor* to the man who was robbed?"

Now it was Jesus who was asking questions. The man answered, "The one who gave him help."

"Then you go and do the same," Jesus told him.

"The same as that Samaritan?" the man thought to himself.

The elders muttered angrily, "What kind of teaching is this? Does this Jesus think Samaritans are better than we?"

Others were angry because Jesus had spoken openly against the priests and the Levites. He had pictured them in the story as men who did wrong in God's sight. He had shown them that a Samaritan might obey God more than a very religious Jew!

Some people said to themselves, "We need to think about this story. Does God want us to love all people? Is anyone who is in trouble *my neighbor?*"

Jesus was finished answering questions. He wanted people to think about the story of the Good Samaritan and find the answer themselves.

This was a new kind of teaching and a new kind of teacher. Anyone who followed Jesus had to change his ways of thinking and living. Word spread through all the country that a man called Jesus was disturbing the people. He taught about God's love for all people. He taught that anyone who followed him must love all people, too.

People had to choose. They had to choose to follow Jesus or to follow their old ways of thinking and living. They had to decide whether Jesus was the most important person in the world for them.

No one knows what the man who asked the questions decided. Maybe he went home to think about Jesus. Maybe he decided that this was the man he should follow and serve.

Or maybe he sided with the enemies of Jesus.

People had to make up their minds about Jesus. The disciples of Jesus had already decided. They had decided to follow Jesus always. They loved Jesus. They wanted to serve him as the One God had sent to make his promises come true. Even though they could not understand Jesus, they loved him.

It was an exciting thing to be a follower of Jesus.

It could also be a dangerous thing.

22. *Uproar in the Synagogue*

Wherever Jesus went crowds of people gathered around him. There was not a village where no one knew him. People in Nazareth knew Jesus the carpenter-teacher, of course. They had been his neighbors. In the brown hills of Judea and under the date palms at Jericho people talked about Jesus. Far to the north where the salt water of the Great Sea washed up on the sand people in Tyre and Sidon remembered Jesus. Rich and powerful people, like the Pharisees and Sadducees, took notice of Jesus. Some were friendly. Others became his enemies.

No longer was Jesus an unknown teacher. People were talking about him everywhere.

Where should Jesus go next? Jesus decided to go back to Nazareth, the village where he had grown up. Here he was welcomed by old friends, by aunts and uncles, cousins and brothers. He had worked here with Joseph as a carpenter and builder. He looked again at the houses and barns he had helped to build. It was good to be back home.

When the Sabbath came, Jesus went to the synagogue. This time he was not treated as a carpenter. He was led to a seat of honor. "Sit up front," said the elder.

Everyone crowded into the synagogue to get a look at Jesus.

"You may read the Scriptures today," said the elder.

So Jesus stood before his people. A heavy scroll was lifted from a beautiful chest. Jesus took the scroll and unrolled it to the place he wanted.

Jesus held the book of the prophet Isaiah. He unrolled it until he came near the end. Loudly and plainly he read the words of Isaiah:

"The Spirit of the Lord is upon me,
because he has anointed me to preach good
   news to the poor.
He has sent me to proclaim release
   to the captives
and recovering of sight to the blind,
to set at liberty those who are oppressed,
   to proclaim the acceptable year of the Lord."

When he was finished, Jesus handed the book back to the attendant.

Everyone waited to hear what Jesus would say. They had been waiting a long time to hear Jesus teach in his home village. Finally he began to speak.

"This very day these verses have come true! They have come true while you were listening to them. I am the One God has sent!" Jesus said.

The promises of God come true? On an ordinary Sabbath and in a town like Nazareth? How dare this man say that!

Jesus went on to talk about the promises of God in the Book of Isaiah. God had promised to send his *Servant* to save his people and bring them back to him. Jesus was saying that he was the *Servant* God had promised to send.

Everyone knew about the great promises of God. But they could not believe Jesus. It did not seem possible that what the great prophet Isaiah said could come true in little Nazareth. It did not seem possible that a neighbor and carpenter's son could be the One whom God had promised to send.

One by one the men began to mutter.

"Who does he think he is?"

"Where did he get all this?"

"He's only a carpenter's son. Isn't Mary his mother?"

"James, Joseph, Simon, and Judas are his brothers. I've never heard them say anything like this about Jesus. Or his sisters either."

"How can he dare to talk the way he does?"

No one doubted the promises of God. No one doubted the words of Isaiah. But everyone thought that when God made his promises come true, he would send a glorious person, shining like an angel. They thought he would send a great king to save the people from the Romans.

"He must be crazy," said one of the elders.

Jesus saw how restless the people were. "When a prophet comes, he is honored everywhere. But he is not honored in his own country," he said sadly.

Jesus went on to tell the people how, long ago, the great Elijah had come. The people of Israel did not welcome him either. Instead he was sent to a widow who lived outside of Israel.

Now the people became angry. They began to shout at Jesus. They rushed up to drive him out of the synagogue. They had honored Jesus, and now he was scolding them. How dare he expect them to believe that the Scriptures were coming true in him!

The strongest men grabbed Jesus and pulled him out the door. Shouting and shaking their fists, they rushed down the village street.

"Take him to the cliff!"

"Throw him down and get rid of him!"

No one could help Jesus. The disciples could not get near him. But when the crowd came to the edge of the cliff, a strange thing happened. No one dared touch Jesus or push him over. Instead, Jesus quietly walked away.

This was the last time he saw his home village. How sad Jesus was! His own people had refused to listen. They had almost put him to death.

The disciples hurried to find Jesus in the hills. As they went, they talked about the great danger to Jesus. They remembered

how the king had arrested John the Baptist and put him in prison.
Might something like this happen to Jesus?

MESSENGERS FROM JOHN THE BAPTIST

Once John the Baptist had been sure that God's promises
were coming true in Jesus. He had pointed to Jesus and said,
"He is the One sent by God. He is far greater than I."

Now John was not so sure. He had been put into prison.
He was very discouraged. Was he right in what he had first said
about Jesus? Finally John sent his friends to ask Jesus, "Are you
the One who was to come, or are we to look for someone else?"

Jesus was sad to hear that John was still in prison. He was
sadder to hear that John was not sure Jesus was the Messiah.
Jesus answered John's question in a strange way. "Tell John
what you have seen me do," he said. "Tell John that the blind
are receiving their sight. Cripples are walking again. Lepers
are being healed. The good news is being brought to the poor."

Then Jesus said, "Happy are those who do not lose faith
in me."

The messengers hurried back to tell John all that they had
seen and heard. But John the Baptist did not have long to
live. Shortly after this, Herod ordered John to be killed.

It was a time of danger for the disciples. It was a time of
danger for anyone who followed Jesus.

Friends hurried to Jesus to tell him what had happened to
John the Baptist. "Be careful," they whispered to him. "The
king may arrest you, too!"

Should Jesus run away? That is what his friends advised him to do.

Instead, Jesus said, "Tell that old fox Herod that I will keep on doing my work today, and tomorrow, and the next day. It will never do for a prophet to meet his death outside of Jerusalem."

These were strange words. The disciples could not understand them at the time. But they knew that Jesus was not afraid.

"We will stay with him," they agreed.

Everywhere people asked, "Who is this man?"

Even the king heard about Jesus. He was worried. "Maybe that man from Nazareth is Elijah come back to life. Maybe he is really John the Baptist," the king said.

Back in Nazareth the people wondered, too. "Is he really the man God promised to send? Or is he a pretender?"

There was no doubt about it. Jesus was a disturbing teacher.

Part 8

Jesus, Our Savior

23. Who Is Jesus of Nazareth?

Even when Jesus went into the hills, the crowds followed him. Sometimes thousands of people followed the wilderness trails to be with Jesus. Every day was a busy one. At times there were so many people around Jesus that the disciples could hardly talk to him.

One day Jesus and his disciples started walking north and left the hills of Galilee behind them. They crossed the border, going beyond the land of the Jews.

"Where are we going?" the disciples wondered.

It was strange to be in villages where everyone spoke a different language. They did not know Jesus.

It was a cool and beautiful land. Clear, cold water bubbled in the many springs, and the countryside was green with trees and orchards. It was the country of Caesarea Philippi.

Perhaps it was on a mountain that Jesus stopped with his disciples. Now there was plenty of time to talk and to think. The disciples could ask questions. But now they felt shy. Not even Peter, who usually did so much talking, knew just what to ask Jesus.

Then Jesus turned to the disciples and asked them a question.

"Who do people say that I am?"

It was easy to tell Jesus what other people thought about him. All the disciples started talking at once. They told Jesus what people in the villages of Galilee had been saying. When people talked about Jesus, they had to decide who he was.

Many people thought that Jesus was another prophet. Except for John, there had not been any prophets for many centuries. People praised God that a new prophet had come. Some people compared Jesus to Jeremiah. Some thought he was Elijah come back to earth again. Some thought he was another John the Baptist.

There seemed no end to the stories which the disciples could tell about what people had been saying. Finally Jesus held up his hand for silence.

Smiling, he asked a new question.

"Who do you say that I am?"

This was different. Now the disciples had to make up their own minds. They were quiet for a while. Each one thought to himself, "What shall I say?" Each one was waiting for someone else to speak.

Who Is Jesus of Nazareth?

Finally Peter stood up bravely. He would say aloud what he had been afraid to say before.

"You are the Christ, the Son of the living God!"

This was a tremendous thing for Peter to say. As a Jew, he had always thought of the Messiah as great and far away. Now he was saying, "You are the Messiah. You are the *Servant* God has sent. You are God's own Son."

This was a happy moment for Jesus. "Blessed are you Simon, son of Jonas," he said. "God has helped you to know and say what you said."

Jesus drew the twelve close together around himself. He explained that they should tell nobody what Peter had said. They should not tell anyone that Jesus was the Messiah—not for a time. People would misunderstand. They expected a different kind of Messiah.

Then Jesus became very sad. He began to tell the disciples that he would have to go back to the crowds in the villages. He would have to go to the great city of Jerusalem. He even said that his enemies would capture him and kill him.

Peter protested. "This must not happen to you!" he declared.

Peter could not imagine a Messiah who would have to die. This was more than the disciples could understand.

Jesus heard what Peter said. He frowned. This was what the Devil wanted—to turn him away from going down to the city of Jerusalem. "Get away from me, Satan!" said Jesus harshly.

JESUS, OUR SAVIOR

Long ago, the Devil had tempted Jesus in the wilderness. Now he was back at work again. Again Satan failed.

Peter was shocked at Jesus' tone of voice. The disciples objected. They did not know how important it was for Jesus to go back to Jerusalem soon. They did not understand how God was making his promises come true.

All Peter knew was that he loved Jesus. He and the disciples wanted to stay with Jesus and help him in any way they could.

24. Friends and Enemies near Jerusalem

In the village of Bethany near Jerusalem, two sisters, Martha and Mary, lived with their brother, Lazarus. One day Martha heard a knock at the door. She hurried to open it, and there stood Jesus. With a cry of joy Martha welcomed her friend.

"Come and sit under our fig tree in the courtyard," she said.

Martha hurried to get Jesus a drink of cold water. There were many things to do—bring water for washing Jesus' feet, sweep the room, build a fire in the oven, make dough, look after the chickens. While Martha was bustling around, Mary sat quietly in the shade. She was listening carefully to everything Jesus said.

Finally Martha could stand it no longer. She came into the courtyard with her hands on her hips.

"Lord, don't you care that I have all the work to do?" she said crossly. "Tell Mary to help me."

Mary blushed and looked down at the ground. Jesus looked at both sisters. Then he said quietly, "Martha, Martha, you worry about so many things. Really, only one thing is important, and Mary has chosen it. What she has, no one can take away from her."

The house of Mary and Martha was a friendly place for Jesus. On his travels through Judea he had stopped here before to be with friends. Then Jesus would go on, perhaps to Jerusalem, perhaps down the hills to Jericho. Mary and Martha could stand on the roof and watch their friend until he was out of sight down the road.

WHEN LAZARUS DIED

One night a lamp burned late in the house in Bethany. Lazarus was sick. The two sisters took turns sitting at his bedside, but he did not get better.

"If only Jesus were here," Mary said.

As soon as the sun rose, Martha sent a neighbor to find Jesus. "Hurry, hurry!" she said. "Lazarus is growing weaker."

Jesus was about a day's journey from Bethany. If he hurried he could get to Lazarus before it was too late. Instead, Jesus did a strange thing. He did not hurry back with the messenger, but spent two more days in the town. The disciples were glad. They thought, "It will be dangerous for Jesus to go anywhere near Jerusalem. The powerful Pharisees in Jerusalem

JESUS, OUR SAVIOR

are talking about stoning Jesus to death. They think he is a blasphemer.''

Two days later Jesus got ready to travel. "Our friend Lazarus has fallen asleep, but I go to wake him out of sleep,'' he said.

Again the disciples could not understand. "If he is sleeping, he'll get well,'' they said.

They did not understand that Jesus really meant that Lazarus was dead.

When Jesus came to Bethany, Lazarus had been dead for four days. His body had been wrapped tightly in grave-clothes and laid in a cave. The door had been sealed with a great stone.

Martha saw Jesus far down the road. She hurried down from the roof and ran to meet Jesus.

"If only you had come earlier," she wept.

Martha could not understand what Jesus meant when he said, "Your brother will live again. I am the resurrection and the life."

Martha ran back to fetch Mary. The two sisters hurried to Jesus. A crowd gathered. They saw how Jesus wept when he talked to the two women. Then Jesus went with them to the grave.

"Roll the stone away," Jesus ordered.

The people did not want to do it. The body was beginning to decay. It had been in the tomb a long time. Jesus insisted, and the men dragged the stone away.

Jesus stood and lifted his arms to pray. Then, when he had finished his prayer, he shouted in a loud voice, "Lazarus! Come out!"

A fearful and wonderful thing happened. A stiff, tightly-wrapped form appeared at the door of the tomb. It was Lazarus! People ran to loosen the grave-clothes. Lazarus was alive and well!

JESUS, OUR SAVIOR

The excitement in the village was great. Some people praised God for the wonderful deeds of Jesus. One would think that the great deed of Jesus would convince everybody. Now everyone would see that the promises of God were coming true! Instead, Jesus made more enemies.

"We must have him put to death," whispered the priests and Pharisees. "That man is too dangerous for us."

They were afraid that Jesus might start a revolution. Then the Roman soldiers would come and destroy Jerusalem.

They hated Jesus because the people listened to him more than to the priests.

Friends of Jesus warned him about his enemies. And Jesus hurried away from Bethany into the wilderness.

Friends and Enemies near Jerusalem

25. Hosanna! Hosanna!

Each time Martha baked bread she saved a pinch of dough. It was a gray-white, soft thing and she put it in a special box. The next time she baked, she would put it into the new dough. This was the leaven that made the bread rise.

At a certain time of the year everyone threw away all the old leaven. No old leaven was allowed to be in the house during the Passover celebration. Every housewife cleaned and scrubbed, swept and dusted. Each dish and pot and spoon was polished.

Martha took her best clothes out of the chest and hung them in the sun. As she worked she sang praises to God. Soon many people would be coming. They would take the road through Bethany toward the stone gates of Jerusalem. They would be on their way to celebrate the great festival in the Temple. Thousands would crowd into the city.

Some people said that Jesus was coming. But others said he would not come for fear of the Pharisees and priests. Martha did not know it, but while she was cleaning house, Jesus had already come as far as Jericho. There he healed blind Bartimaeus. In Jericho he invited himself to the house of Zacchaeus and astonished both that tax collector and the people.

The next day the news spread like wildfire from one end of Bethany to the other. "Jesus is coming! All twelve disciples are with him! He is coming to Jerusalem for the Passover!"

From far away Martha could hear the pilgrims singing a psalm which they always sang on the way to Jerusalem for the Passover.

"O give thanks to the LORD, for he is good;
   his steadfast love endures for ever!"

Everyone in the village was ready to join them. They were only waiting for news about Jesus.

"He is in Bethphage!" shouted a man and pointed to the nearby village.

More and more people hurried to see Jesus. The sun shone. Flowers bloomed, for the hot wind of summer had not yet come to wither them.

"He's on a donkey! Hail to our Jesus!"

Someone carried a long palm branch and waved it to and fro in time to the singing.

Soon there were hundreds of palm branches waving like tall, green flags.

Men took off their cloaks and laid them on the path, like a carpet for a king. Children brought flowers to hang around the donkey's neck. They would be jewels for the king.

Hosanna! Hosanna!

"Open to me the gates of righteousness,
    that I may enter through them
    and give thanks to the LORD."

The people were singing Psalm 118. As they sang, they thought
of God's promises to help them. They thought how, long ago,
he had sent Moses to lead them out of the land of Egypt. They
thought about Joshua and how he led the children of Israel into
the promised land. They thought of the prophet Zechariah,
who had declared many centuries ago:

"Rejoice greatly, O daughter of Zion!
    Shout aloud, O daughter of Jerusalem!

JESUS, OUR SAVIOR

Lo, your king comes to you;
  triumphant and victorious is he,
humble and riding on an ass,
  on a colt the foal of an ass."

First one voice took up the words, "Hosanna! Hosanna!"
Soon everyone was singing,

  "Hosanna to the Son of David!
    Blessed be he who comes in the name of the Lord!
  Hosanna in the highest."

Jesus rode on. He smiled at the happy children. He smiled
at the happy disciples. He rode on toward the city, for he was

indeed the "Son of David" and the One whom God had sent to fulfill his promises.

As the joyous crowd crossed the Kidron Brook and looked up to the gates of Jerusalem, the people of Bethany took up a new chant.

"Make way for the King!" someone shouted. "The King is coming!"

"God bless the King, the Son of David," the people sang.

"Blessed is he who comes in the name of the Lord," sang the people of Bethany.

When the procession reached the gate to the city, a crowd was waiting. "Who is this man?" people in Jerusalem asked.

"Jesus the prophet, the man from Nazareth in Galilee," the people answered.

In the Temple courtyard the chief priests and elders whispered together. "What are we going to do with this man? The whole world is running after him."

As they whispered, they heard the hosannas of the crowd. But neither the priests nor the crowd knew who Jesus really was. The time had not yet come for that.

26. Monday to Thursday in Jerusalem

The Temple in Jerusalem was like a large outdoor church. Inside the gate there was a large, square courtyard. It was big enough for thousands of people. Around the sides were tall marble pillars. They held up the roof of the long porches, where people could gather in the shade. In the center of the courtyard was a raised platform for the altar. This was where the priests made the great sacrifices. Behind the altar stood the Holy of Holies building.

People came and went across the Temple courtyard every day. Thousands of them could see Jesus there. He spoke boldly in the shade of the Temple porch. This troubled the priests and Pharisees greatly. They wanted to kill Jesus and he was there right under their noses. But they did not dare to arrest him. The happy crowds would not permit that.

Jesus looked around the Temple fearlessly. He saw pens of sheep and cages of pigeons, and booths for the money changers. Jesus was angry. He drove all of these merchants out of the Temple courtyard.

"My house shall be called a house of prayer," Jesus said.

Now the priests would have to take notice, but they were afraid to arrest Jesus. So the elders and the priests decided to attack Jesus with words. They sent their best men to ask Jesus questions and to trap him in arguments.

"Who gave you the right to do what you are doing?" they demanded.

"I'll tell you who gave it to me," Jesus said, "if you will answer one question for me. Did John get his right to baptize people from heaven or from earth?"

This was a question the elders were not ready to answer. They walked away into a room where they could discuss the matter alone.

"What can we say?" they wondered. "If we say John got his right from heaven, the people will tell us we should have believed John. We should have been baptized ourselves. But if we say John's right came from men on earth, think what the crowd might do to us! They believe that John was a true prophet of God."

Finally the elders came back and shook their heads.

"We do not know," they said.

"Then I will not tell you by what right I preach and teach," Jesus told them.

Jesus went on telling story after story to show the elders that they had displeased God by refusing to accept John and, now, Jesus himself. He told the story of a farmer who planted a vineyard. The farmer rented the vineyard to some workers. Then he went on a journey to a distant country. When harvest time came, he sent a servant to get his share of the harvest. The workers beat the servant and sent him back empty-handed. The farmer tried again to get his share of the harvest. Again the workers treated the servant shamefully. Finally the farmer decided to send his own son. "They will listen to him," he thought. But the workers killed the son and threw his body out of the vineyard.

At the end of his story Jesus asked, "What should the owner do now?"

"He should come and punish those workers in a terrible way," the people answered.

The elders and priests understood Jesus. They were furious because Jesus compared them to the wicked people in the story. God had taken care of Israel as lovingly as a farmer cares for his vineyard. He had given his great promises to Israel. Then there was a long time of waiting. He sent his servants—the prophets—but the people refused to listen. Then he sent his Son. . . .

The priests tried again and again to trap Jesus with clever questions. Once they asked Jesus if it were right to pay taxes to Rome. If Jesus said, "Yes," they could turn the people against him. Every Jew hated to pay taxes to Caesar. If Jesus said,

"No," the priests could complain to the Romans and say, "This man is dangerous. He is telling the people not to pay taxes."

Like all the other traps, this one failed, too. Jesus asked for a coin. "Look at the picture on it," he said. "Who is that person?"

There was only one answer. It was a picture of Caesar, the Roman emperor.

"Then pay to Caesar what belongs to him, and give to God what belongs to him," Jesus said.

Every day that week from Monday to Thursday Jesus taught in the Temple. No one dared harm him because the crowds praised God for this great teacher.

"The kingdom of God is going to be taken away from you," Jesus warned the rulers of the Temple.

The rulers met secretly. They decided that they must get rid of Jesus. "If we don't do anything, he will turn all the people against us," they said.

As they plotted and planned, Jesus spoke even more boldly. He turned to the scribes and Pharisees and declared, "You are hypocrites. You pretend to be holy, but inside you are not. You are like the graves of the dead. They are painted white on the outside so that they look clean. But inside they are full of dead men's bones. You say, 'What a terrible thing that our ancestors did when they stoned the prophets!' And yet you are doing the same thing!"

Now the scribes and Pharisees were furious. They did not know what to do. Then a strange thing happened. Judas Iscariot, one of the twelve disciples, came and said that he would help them. He would lead them to where Jesus stayed at night. Then they could arrest Jesus secretly when there were no crowds to protect him. The priests were delighted. They paid Judas thirty pieces of silver for his help.

"We must act quickly," the priests said. "This must be done before the festival begins."

ON THURSDAY EVENING

The day for the Passover meal was coming nearer. On that day people would gather to eat roast lamb and to celebrate the day of deliverance from Egypt. Jesus wanted to eat the Passover meal with his disciples. He decided to eat the Passover meal on Thursday in Jerusalem.

"Go to Jerusalem," Jesus told his disciples. "When you see a man carrying a pitcher of water, follow him." A man would be easy to notice because usually only women carried water.

Jesus gave other secret instructions. "Follow the man to the house where he goes and say to the owner of the house, 'The Master says, "Where is the room for me to eat the Passover?"' He will show you a large room that will have everything we need. Get things ready for our Passover."

The disciples did this secretly so that none of Jesus' enemies would know where he was. Jesus wanted a quiet time

JESUS, OUR SAVIOR

with only the twelve disciples near him. The disciples did not know that this would be their last meal with him before he died.

The Passover was a happy festival. There was feasting and singing. Everyone had a good time. Children ate roast lamb with their parents and heard again the stories of God's great deeds.

For Jesus and the disciples this Passover meal was quiet and sad.

During the meal Jesus looked at Judas and said to the disciples, "One of you is going to betray me."

The disciples were already worried about Jesus. They knew that powerful people in Jerusalem had turned against Jesus. But how could Jesus think they would ever do anything to harm him!

"Surely you do not mean one of us?" they asked him in alarm.

One after another they asked the terrible question, "Am I the one?"

"It is one of you," Jesus said sorrowfully. "It is written in the Scriptures that this will happen but I feel very sorry for the one who will do it. It would have been better if he had never been born."

Fearfully Judas Iscariot asked, "Is it I, Master?"

Jesus dipped his bread into the dish and said very quietly, "It is the one to whom I give this bread." Then he gave the bread to Judas. "Go and be quick about your business," he said.

Judas slipped out into the dark. The others thought he was doing an errand. They did not know what evil thoughts were in Judas' mind.

At every Passover meal the head of the table would take the bread and pass it around. He would do the same with the goblets of wine. When Jesus did this, he did it in a way that the disciples never forgot.

Jesus took the bread. He prayed the usual prayer. Then he

broke the crisp loaves of bread in pieces and shared them with his followers.

"Take and eat," he said. "This is my body."

When the time came to pass the goblet of wine, Jesus praised God for the fruit of the vine.

Then he said, "Drink of it, all of you. This is my blood which is shed for you in the new covenant. I will not drink any more wine until I drink it anew in the kingdom of God."

There was a terrible silence in the Upper Room. The disciples knew that something very important was happening. What was Jesus telling them? What did it mean, "bread . . . my body? Wine . . . my blood"?

The disciples whispered among themselves. Some sat in silence, thinking. Jesus' eyes were very sad. And so they asked no questions at this time.

After the meal Jesus looked at the eleven disciples. "You will all leave me," he said.

Peter protested. He was sure that he would never leave his Master. "Even if everyone else loses faith," Peter declared, "I never will."

"Peter," said Jesus, "before the rooster crows in the morning, you will deny me three times."

"Even if I have to die with you, I will never say I do not know you!" Peter insisted.

The meal was over. It was late. The disciples got up and sang a hymn of praise. Then they went out into the dark, through the silent streets of Jerusalem.

27. Arrested . . . Condemned . . . Crucified

Near Jerusalem on the way to Bethany there was an olive grove. The Hebrew name for this olive grove was *Gethsemane*. Jesus liked Gethsemane because it was a quiet and beautiful place.

On Thursday evening he took his disciples to the gate of this grove. Jesus pointed to three disciples—Peter, James, and John. "Come away from the others. Stay with me while I pray," he said. "I cannot go on much longer," Jesus said. "My heart is full of sorrow." While the other disciples sat down to rest and to sleep, Jesus and the three walked into the grove and disappeared among the shadows of the trees.

The disciples were used to this. Often, when Jesus had to make an important decision, he spent hours in prayer. This time Jesus was more troubled than they had ever seen him.

The four went to a quiet, hidden place in the grove. The great rocks were still warm from the sun. Peter, James, and John sat down. They were tired. Soon they were stretched out comfortably, near the stones. Their heads nodded, and they closed their eyes. Jesus went a few steps away to pray. When he came back, the three were sound asleep. "Couldn't you stay awake just one hour?" he asked Peter.

Jesus went away a second time. The disciples could hear him praying. "Father," he sighed. "Father, all things are possible to thee. Take away this cup of suffering from me. Yet not what I will but what thou wilt."

The minutes went by. The disciples could not keep their eyes open. Finally they slipped off to sleep again.

Again Jesus returned and shook them awake. They were so sleepy they did not know what to say.

For a third time Jesus went away to pray. When he returned, again he found them sleeping. He spoke with a firm, clear voice, "Get up. Let us be going. My betrayer is coming near."

Sleepily the disciples followed Jesus to the stone gate. There they saw lights moving up and down. They heard a crowd of noisy men tramping up the path to the olive grove. Light from many lanterns gleamed on their swords and clubs. In front of the crowd was a man the disciples recognized. It was Judas Iscariot.

Walking faster then the rest, Judas came straight to Jesus. "Master!" he said and kissed him.

Arrested . . . Condemned . . . Crucified   227

This was not a kiss of friendship. It was a secret signal. The men with clubs and swords rushed at Jesus.

Things happened quickly. Peter drew his sword and swung it around his head. He would rush in and get Jesus free. The men ducked out of the way of the sword, but it slashed at someone's head and cut off an ear.

Jesus spoke to Peter. "That is enough," he commanded.

Jesus touched the man who was wounded and healed his ear. Then he turned to the Temple guards and said, "Why do you come after me with swords? I was in the Temple every day. You could easily find me there."

The disciples began to understand what was happening. Jesus was giving himself up. They could not fight such a large

JESUS, OUR SAVIOR

crowd. Suddenly they were frightened and ran away to hide. Jesus was left alone. He did not move as the men twisted a rope hard and tight around his arms.

CONDEMNED TO DEATH

It was dark in Jerusalem. Most people had gone to bed. The city was quiet, but hundreds of lamps were burning in the courtyard of the high priest's palace. Men came and went. The council of elders gathered to hear the case against Jesus. They would have to act quickly, for it would be too late when the festival began.

According to Jewish law, a man could not be condemned to death unless there were proof that he had done wrong. At least two witnesses had to be found to prove his crime. What one witness said had to agree exactly with what the other said. The priests found some men who were willing to tell lies against Jesus. They got ready for the midnight trial.

"Here they come!" a guard shouted. "I can see the torches."

A man came to the steps with a rope in his hand. At the other end of the rope walked Jesus.

"Who is that man?" some people asked. "He walks as quietly as a sheep led to slaughter."

The guard brought Jesus into the palace. All the men of the high council stared at him. Jesus stood alone. Quickly false witnesses were brought before the high priest.

First one man told his story. Then the other man spoke. But what the second man said did not agree with the first man's story. The priests were angry. Their plot had failed. Anyone could see that these were false witnesses.

Others shouted from the crowd. "We heard him say, 'I can pull down the Temple of God and build it up in three days!'"

The high priest had heard enough. He jumped to his feet and shouted at Jesus, "Why don't you say something? Answer! Are these men telling the truth?"

Jesus did not say a word. The high priest was furious. His lips foamed with anger.

"I command you by the living God," he roared. "Tell the truth. Are you the Christ, the Son of God?"

"You have said so," answered Jesus quietly.

The high priest tore his robe. That was the way the Jews showed grief or sorrow. He acted as if Jesus had said something insulting against God. He turned to the council and said in a hoarse voice, "What is your verdict?"

The men of the council answered, "He deserves to die."

But not everyone spoke. Some bowed their heads in silence. They were secret followers of Jesus. But they were afraid to speak up for him.

The words of the council were a signal to those around Jesus. They slapped him and mocked him. The guards beat him with their fists as they pushed him out of the room.

PETER'S DENIAL

One disciple who ran away came back to see where the men were taking Jesus. It was Peter. Hiding in the shadows, he followed the torches as far as the palace. Peter hesitated. Then he slipped into the courtyard. He stood in the back with the servants and hoped that no one would notice him. It was chilly, so Peter edged his way toward the fire to keep warm. Once in a while torchlight flickered over his face. But Peter was sure no one recognized him.

A servant crossed the courtyard several times. She looked at Peter and wondered who he was. "Weren't you with Jesus, the man from Galilee?" she asked him.

Peter did not dare give himself away. "I don't know what you are talking about," he said. He got up and hurried away.

A woman saw Peter and said, "Look, this man was with Jesus of Nazareth."

Again Peter said even more loudly, "I do not even know the man!" More people gathered around him and looked at his face in the shadows.

"Oh, come now, we know you are one of them. You are a Galilean yourself!"

This time Peter began to curse and swear that he did not know Jesus. Then from far away Peter heard the thin, shrill crowing of a rooster. Peter shrank back. He remembered! The words of Jesus rang in his ears, "Before the rooster crows . . ."

Peter ran out through the gate. Tears blinded his eyes. His shoulders shook with sobs. He walked alone as the first soft streaks of dawn broke across the night sky. The torches in the palace sputtered out, and the fire in the court sank to a circle of ashes. It was the end of a terrible night.

TRIAL BEFORE PILATE

In the morning Jesus was marched through the streets of Jerusalem. His face was bruised and dirty. He could not even wipe off the dirt because his hands were tied like a criminal's. People crowded the streets on their way to buy food for the feast day before the beginning of the Sabbath that evening. Some followed along to see what would happen next. Others hurried away. They were afraid. They did not want anyone to know that they had once listened to Jesus and sung praises about him.

"It is safer to pretend we were not there when he came into the city," they whispered. They did not want to be arrested. They did not want to be brought to court as witnesses.

Jesus walked with quiet dignity. His guards took him to the great palace of the Roman governor, but they stayed outside. No Jew wanted to go into such a house. That would make him unclean for the holy days of the Passover festival.

"Will there be time enough?" wondered the priests and Pharisees. At six o'clock the Sabbath would begin. Then no one could be put to death.

One of the elders banged his fist on the door. He called for Pilate, the Roman governor, to come outside. He demanded that Pilate hold the trial right there, out on the porch.

A servant came and then disappeared. After a while other servants came. They were carrying a heavy gold chair. They set it near the wide marble steps. Soldiers stood on both sides. Then Pilate walked out. He wore a soft, white toga—the robe of an elegant Roman official. At once the crowd cheered.

"Hail to Pilate," they cried. "Hail to Caesar's governor."

Pilate frowned. He did not like the Jews. He knew they hated him. He was suspicious. Something was wrong. Then Pilate looked at the weary and bruised prisoner.

Everyone began talking at once. Pilate could catch only a few words. ". . . Misleading our nation. . . . Forbidding us to pay taxes. . . . Dangerous! . . . Troublemaker! . . . Calls himself a king!"

At the word *king*, Pilate raised his eyebrows. If there were anyone the Romans feared, it was someone who might claim to be king and start a revolution.

Pilate held up his hands and asked the crowd to be quiet. He turned to the prisoner, who stood straight and quiet.

"Well," said Pilate, "*are you* the King of the Jews?"

Jesus had been silent. Now his lips parted. He said only a few words, "You have said so."

The priests elbowed their way past the soldiers. They stood in a ring around the white-robed Pilate. The mob came closer. The elders began to yell in Pilate's ear.

"He stirs up the people! He makes trouble everywhere—in Galilee, in Judea!"

Pilate scratched his head. He was undecided. He looked at Jesus again. Pilate did not think he was a dangerous man. Then he looked at the priests and elders. They were in an ugly mood, and they could get him, the Roman governor, into trouble. If he could only think of an excuse!

Then Pilate tried a trick. It was the custom to pardon a prisoner on the festival day. He would let the people choose between this innocent man and a criminal who was guilty of murder. Surely the people would choose to have Jesus pardoned. Then the matter would be settled quickly.

Pilate clapped his hands. He gave his orders. Soon the powerful figure of Barabbas appeared between two guards.

Barabbas was a dangerous criminal, a murderer.

"Which one shall I set free?" Pilate asked.

While this was going on, the priests and elders darted around in the crowd, whispering into one ear and another. There was a roar from the crowd. To his surprise, Pilate heard the word, "Bar-ab-bas!"

Pilate would not give up. "What shall I do with Jesus, who is called the Christ?" he asked weakly.

The people in the crowd rocked back and forth. Over and over again they shouted, "Cru-ci-fy. . . . Cru-ci-fy!"

Pilate was horrified. Should he allow an innocent man to be tortured to death? There seemed no way out. He was afraid to back down. A riot might start at any time. Solemnly he ordered a bowl of water to be brought. He washed his hands as the crowd watched.

"I am not to blame for this man's death," he said. "You must take the blame!"

The guards let Barabbas go. They tied Jesus to a pillar. Then they took whips and lashed his back. This was always done before a traitor was crucified. This was the Roman way to punish a traitor.

Someone twisted some thorns into a crown and slapped it on Jesus' head. The soldiers laughed and pretended Jesus was a king. One handed Jesus a bent reed.

"Your scepter, your majesty," he said.

They made Jesus drag the heavy beams of the cross through the cobblestone streets. The procession moved slowly as the cross bumped over the stones. Everyone knew where they were going. Outside the city was a place that looked like a rubbish heap. It was called Golgotha, which means "hill of the skull." No flowers grew here. No trees offered shade. High in the sky, vultures circled.

CRUCIFIED

From far away the disciples heard the noise of the soldiers. They heard the shrill screams of the crowd as three crosses rose into the sky. They could not bear to look at the naked

men who hung there to die. In silent sorrow and despair the disciples wept.

Others ran out to jeer and mock. They asked why Jesus did not try to save himself if he were really the King of the Jews. Some women crept nearer. They pulled their veils over their faces and watched in silence. Jesus lifted his head. He was trying to speak. For a moment the crowd fell silent.

"Father," he said. "Forgive them. They do not know what they are doing."

Slowly, too slowly, the sun moved across the sky. Noon-

JESUS, OUR SAVIOR

time had passed. Then a great darkness spread over the city.
People stopped laughing and mocking Jesus. Some were afraid
and ran to their homes. Others waited in curious silence.

In the stillness that followed, Jesus cried, "Father, I com-
mend my spirit into your hands."

There, on the "hill of the skull," between two criminals,
Jesus died. Even the soldiers were shocked and amazed. Their
captain, a centurion, looked up at Jesus and said, "Truly this
man was the Son of God!"

What he said meant far more than he could know.

Arrested . . . Condemned . . . Crucified

28. The Risen Lord

Peter heard a soft knock at the door. The door was locked and barred. Again Peter heard the knocking. He looked out through a crack between the planks, but he could not see who it was. Then he heard a low whistle. It was his brother Andrew. Quickly he unbarred the door. Andrew slipped in and helped close the door.

One by one the disciples and friends of Jesus came to the secret room. Peter's eyes were red with weariness and his shoulders sagged. James and John sat together in silence. They were thinking about how they had folded up their fishing nets and left everything to follow Jesus. Now he was dead. And they were left alone, like sheep without a shepherd.

It was the Sabbath. The followers of Jesus huddled together in the little room. They could not celebrate with the crowds in Jerusalem. They did not dare go to the Temple for the sacrifices. Even though the door was closed, they talked in whispers. The disciples were confused and afraid.

"Six days ago the people sang praises to him," said one of the women. Like the others, she was trying to understand the awful thing that had happened.

" 'Hail to the King,' they were shouting then," another disciple murmured.

Each disciple had his own secret thoughts. Matthew wondered what he should do. Could he go back to collecting taxes? Andrew thought sadly of the day when he leaped into Peter's boat with the good news about Jesus. Should he go back to Galilee?

Another disciple thought about Judas. He had heard that Judas had killed himself.

It was a day of waiting and wondering and weeping. It was a long, silent Sabbath that stretched into a longer night. Without sleep and without hope, Jesus' friends waited for the morning.

Slowly the light of dawn unwrapped the darkness of the night. It was like an angel taking away the blackness of death. Mary from Magdala watched the morning come. She had a plan.

"They will not harm a woman," she whispered. "I know where they put him."

Mary and the other women had made plans to go to the tomb of Jesus as soon as it was light. They would take sweet-smelling spices to lay on the body of Jesus.

While the women were on their way to the tomb, an amazing and terrifying thing happened. The ground shook with an earthquake. The guards at the tomb trembled with fear. An angel in blazing white rolled away the heavy stone in front of the burial cave.

When the women came to the open grave they did not understand what had happened. They were afraid and surprised, astonished and shocked at the same time. Mary fell to her knees.

She looked into the tomb. It was empty! Some of the women saw the angel and heard him say, "Don't be afraid. I know you are looking for Jesus, who was crucified. He is not here. He is alive as he said. Look; see for yourself that he is gone. Then go quickly, and tell his disciples that he has risen from the dead."

The women ran back to the secret room where the disciples were hiding. Each had a story to tell. In their excitement they all spoke at once. "He is alive . . . just as he said!"

The disciples could not believe what the women said. They did not know what to think. But on the evening of that same day the disciples themselves saw Jesus and talked to him. He appeared in their secret room. Then the disciples were full of joy. Their fears were swept away as the sun drives away the darkness of night.

Slowly the disciples remembered what Jesus had said long ago about himself and what would happen in Jerusalem. Truly Jesus was the Son of God. His death on the cross was not the

end. It was part of God's wonderful plan! The kingdom of God was near and real because Jesus was their Lord, their risen Lord.

Other disciples had seen Jesus at Emmaus. Some saw him again in Galilee. Jesus gave his disciples a great task to do.

"Go and make disciples of all nations," he told them. "Baptize them in the name of the Father and of the Son and of the Holy Spirit. Teach them to live as I have taught you. Remember! I will be with you always, even to the end of the world."

Jesus the Christ, the Son of the living God, was their Lord. He had called them to tell all men the good news of a risen Lord. With this word of promise and command Jesus left his disciples. His work on earth was finished. He had done what God wanted him to do.

The disciples went back to Jerusalem. They went back to wait for the power Jesus promised would come to them. They were prepared to serve and obey their Christ, who would be with them everywhere.

Part 9

Men of Pentecost

29. *"You Shall Be My Witnesses"*

Luke's eyes glowed with excitement. His pen moved swiftly over the new page of papyrus. What an amazing story he had to tell Theophilus!

"In the first book, O Theophilus," Luke wrote, "I told you all that Jesus began to do and teach."

More than anything else, Luke had wanted Theophilus to know the truth about Jesus and his followers. Already he had written a full scroll to tell all he had learned about Jesus. He had told Theophilus the stories Christians liked to tell of the night when the Son of God was born in a stable in Bethlehem. Luke had told how Jesus went about bringing to poor and unhappy people the good news that God was near to help them. He told how Jesus had said that God is like a loving Father who is glad when his runaway child comes home again. He is like a good shepherd who searches for one lost sheep until he finds it and brings it back safely to the fold. Then

Luke had written a long story of how angry men had put Jesus to death on a cross. But three days later Jesus' followers had seen him alive again!

All these things Luke had written in his first book. But he had more to tell Theophilus—much more! The story he was writing now was so exciting that he could not keep still about it. It was the story of how God had helped people like Luke know what Jesus had done for them. It was the story of brave witnesses who kept on telling about Jesus, even when they knew that they might be put in prison or even killed.

At first there had been only a little group of followers in Jerusalem. Jesus' mother and brothers, eleven disciples, and a few friends—that was all. But now there were so many followers of Jesus that no one could count them! In every land around the Mediterranean Sea there were people who had heard and believed that Jesus was the Savior sent by God. Even in faraway Rome Christians were telling the story of Jesus! How had it all happened? How had it started?

This is the story that Luke remembered and wrote.

Jesus was alive again! The glad news rang in the hearts of Jesus' followers like joyful bells. Alive! Alive! The women had come running from the empty tomb with the news. Then Peter and John and the other disciples had actually seen him! They walked and talked with him again. Now they were sure that all he had told them was true. He was the Christ! He had brought them forgiveness and a new, rich life with God.

For forty days Jesus came to talk with his disciples. He answered their questions. He taught them more about the kingdom of God.

"You are *witnesses*," he told them. "You must tell others what you have seen and heard."

Then one day he told them that they would not see him anymore. But he promised to be with them in a new way.

"Wait in Jerusalem," he told the disciples. "Soon my Father will send you the Holy Spirit. When the Holy Spirit comes, he will give you power to tell others about me.

"And you shall be my witnesses in Jerusalem and in all Judea and Samaria and to the end of the earth."

Then, suddenly, Jesus was gone. The disciples knew that they would not talk and walk with him as before. But they were not sad. He was their living Lord and Savior. They felt very close to him, even though they could not see him. And they were sure that someday, perhaps very soon, he would come back to be their king forever.

The disciples went back to Jerusalem. There was work to do. Many people must be told what God had done for them in Jesus. And the followers of Jesus must tell the story.

In Jerusalem the friends of Jesus prayed together. They waited for the Holy Spirit to come as Jesus had promised. How would he come? What would happen next? The followers of Jesus were not sure. But they were sure that something wonderful and exciting was just beginning—something that would change the whole world!

MEN OF PENTECOST

30. Birthday of the Church

The streets of Jerusalem overflowed with holiday travelers. Worshipers jammed the Temple courtyards. From all of Palestine, from far-off Egypt and Africa, from every nation in the Roman world faithful Jews had come to celebrate Pentecost. The streets of the city rang with the sound of many different languages!

Pentecost was the important festival of the wheat harvest. It was always an important time. But nobody guessed how important *this* Pentecost was going to be!

In a house in Jerusalem the disciples of Jesus were waiting and praying together. Suddenly their waiting was over. Suddenly they were sure what they must do, and they were not afraid. They were filled with a strange and very wonderful power!

"When the day of Pentecost had come," Luke wrote to Theophilus, "they were all together in one place. And suddenly a sound came from heaven like the rush of a mighty wind, and it filled all the house where they were sitting. And there appeared to them tongues as of fire . . . resting on each one of them. And they were all filled with the Holy Spirit." The promise of Jesus had come true—the Holy Spirit had come to them.

All the disciples began to speak at once. What a great noise that was to hear! They rushed outside telling everyone that Jesus was the Savior! Soon a crowd gathered around the disciples. And every person who stopped was astonished at what he heard. For the disciples were telling the mighty deeds God had done through Jesus. And every person who listened, no matter what his home language was, heard the disciples talking in his own language!

"How can this be?" they asked each other. "What does it mean? Aren't all these men from Galilee? Then how can each of us understand what they are saying?"

No one could explain it. But some people pointed at the disciples and laughed. "These men are drunk!" they said to each other.

Just then Peter began to speak. "Now listen to me!" he shouted.

Everyone stopped to listen to the fisherman disciple. Even the other disciples were amazed at Peter. Was this the same man who had once been afraid to admit that he was a follower of Jesus? Now he was telling thousands of people about his Lord!

"These men are not drunk," Peter was saying in a strong, clear voice. "They are filled with the Spirit of God!"

Then Peter told the Jews all the wonderful deeds which God had done through Jesus.

"You killed this man Jesus," Peter said, "but God raised him up! He is alive again—and of that we all are witnesses! He is truly the Messiah whom God promised long ago to send us. He is the Christ, the Savior! Even now he is with God. And he has given us his Holy Spirit so that you might know these things."

The Christ! The Messiah! Now the people knew what a terrible thing they had done. They felt ashamed and afraid and alone. What could they ever do to feel right with God again?

"What shall we do?" they asked. "Please tell us what we can do!"

Peter's answer was strong and sure. "Repent and be baptized in the name of Jesus Christ!" he told them. "Because of what Jesus has done, God will forgive your sins. You will receive the gift of the Holy Spirit. This is God's promise to you and to your children, and to all others whom God will call to him."

On that day, three thousand people believed in Jesus and were baptized. The day of Pentecost became the birthday of the church.

31. Brave Witnesses

Everywhere in Jerusalem people were talking about the amazing followers of Jesus:

"Have you ever seen anything like it? They are like one large family. Every person has sold his belongings. They share everything with one another!"

"Every day they are together, praying and eating a special meal, and learning from the apostles."

"I have heard that they are waiting for Jesus to come again."

"Waiting! They are doing more than that! They are telling everyone about this Jesus who died on a cross. Have you heard the apostles preach? Never have I heard such preaching. They say that Jesus is alive again! They say that he is the Messiah sent by God."

"That is not all. They say that those who believe in him

have forgiveness from God. They say that because Jesus lives, everyone who trusts in him will live with God forever!"

"I have heard of great miracles and signs the apostles do."

"But how can that be? They are not educated men like our teachers and scribes. They are just poor fishermen. One was even a tax collector!"

"Aren't these the same men who ran away when their Master was arrested? Why, not so long ago that fisherman from Galilee would not even admit that he knew Jesus! How can these same men be great preachers and miracle workers?"

"I do not know. Something has happened to change them."

It was true. Something had happened to change the disciples. Once they had run away in fear. But now no one was running away. Nothing could stop Peter and the other apostles from preaching and teaching. Every day more people became followers of Jesus. The church in Jerusalem was growing larger and larger.

THE MAN AT THE TEMPLE GATE

One afternoon Peter and John went to the Temple to pray. As they came to the entrance called Beautiful Gate, they saw a man being carried to the Temple. The man could not use his legs. Every day at the hour of prayer friends brought him to beg from people who went in and out. When the lame man saw Peter and John, he stretched out his hands and asked for money.

Peter looked at the man. "I have no silver or gold to give you," he said. "But I will give you what I have. In the name of Jesus Christ of Nazareth—walk!"

The surprised man reached up to take Peter's hand. Peter helped him to his feet. The man stood on his thin legs. It was true! He could walk! Walking and leaping and praising God, he went into the Temple with Peter and John.

When the people saw what had happened, they were astonished. They ran to look at the lame man and Peter and John. Peter knew that this was a chance to tell these people about Jesus.

"Men of Israel, why are you surprised at this?" Peter asked. "Do you think we made this man walk? No! The God of Abraham and Isaac and Jacob has done this—the same God whom Jesus served. And you have killed God's servant Jesus! You shouted for Pilate to let a murderer go free instead of Jesus. Jesus died because of your sin. But God raised him from the dead. To this we are witnesses!"

Then Peter told the people that in Jesus God had kept the promises he had made to Abraham long ago. Through Jesus, God would bless all the world.

Just then, before anyone could whisper a warning to Peter, the priests and the captain of the Temple pushed through the crowd. Behind them came the Sadducees. Everyone could see how angry they were! They wanted no more preaching like that! The guards arrested Peter and John and put them in prison. But many people believed in Jesus that day.

The next day Peter and John were brought before the temple rulers and the high priest.

"Where did you get the power to do this?" the rulers asked.

Then the Holy Spirit helped Peter answer. "Leaders and elders," Peter said, "are you asking us how this man was healed? It was done in the name of Jesus Christ of Nazareth. He is the One you crucified, but God raised him from the dead. Nobody else except Jesus can save us. He is the only way we can come to God."

When the rulers heard this, they asked Peter and John to wait outside.

"How can this be?" the rulers asked one another. "How can ordinary fishermen heal and preach like this?" They did not know what to do with Peter and John.

"They must be punished," someone said.

"But what have they done?" asked one ruler. "We cannot deny that the lame man is healed. Everyone can see that!"

"If we punish them, the crowd may be angry," another said.

"But this must not happen again," they all agreed.

Finally they called Peter and John back. "You may go free this time," they said. "But we warn you: Do not speak about Jesus anymore—not to anyone!"

Peter and John were not afraid. "We cannot help but tell what we have seen and heard," they said.

MEN OF PENTECOST

The disciples were allowed to leave, but they were warned again never to speak of Jesus to anyone. They would get into real trouble if they did!

But when the friends of Peter and John heard what had happened, they asked God to help them. "Almighty Lord," they prayed, "grant to thy servants to speak thy word with all boldness."

And the Holy Spirit helped them to speak even more bravely than before.

32. An Excited City

The high priest was really angry now. These apostles of Jesus were upsetting the whole city! They even dared to preach in the Temple courtyard. And every day more people believed in this Jesus of Nazareth!

That Peter was the worst troublemaker of them all. He wasn't afraid of anything! And the other apostles followed his example. And the people! Now they were even bringing sick people into the street so that Peter's shadow would fall on them as he passed by. The streets were full of beds and pallets. From all the villages around Jerusalem people were bringing sick friends and relatives to be healed. And they were healed! That made the high priest angrier still.

"Arrest these apostles!" he ordered.

So Peter and the other apostles were thrown into prison. But during the night an angel of the Lord opened the prison doors. The apostles were free!

"Go to the Temple," the angel told them. "Tell everyone about the new life Jesus has brought."

In the morning the high priest called the rulers of Israel together. He ordered the apostles brought from the prison.

In a little while the officers returned, looking very frightened. "They aren't there!" they reported. "The prison is locked, and the guards are still on duty. But there isn't anyone inside!"

The palace was in an uproar. No one could understand how such a thing had happened. Where were the apostles?

Finally someone came to tell them, "The men you put in prison are standing in the Temple, teaching the people!"

Then the captain of the Temple and his officers went and brought the apostles before the rulers.

"You have not obeyed my orders," the high priest said angrily. "I told you to stop teaching in Jesus' name. And now look what you have done! You have filled all Jerusalem with your teaching. You are trying to blame us for that man's death."

Peter spoke for all the apostles. "We must obey God rather than men," he said. "God raised up Jesus after you killed him. He has made Jesus Leader and Savior, so that everyone in Israel—even you—can repent and be forgiven of all your sins. We are witnesses to all this. And so is the Holy Spirit, whom God has given to those who obey him."

This made the rulers of Israel so angry that they wanted to kill the apostles.

"Put them to death!" some shouted. "Get rid of them before they make fools of us before the whole city!"

One man had said nothing at all. He was Gamaliel, a famous teacher of the Law. Now he held up his hand for silence. The room became quiet.

"Take the apostles outside," Gamaliel said.

Then he turned to the rulers of Israel. "Be careful what you do with these men," he warned. "Let them alone. If this teaching is just their own idea, it won't last long. It will fail by itself. But if this is really God's teaching, you will not be able to stop them. You might even find that you are actually fighting against God!"

The rulers of Israel were frightened. Suppose what the apostles said was really true! They had not thought of that. They did not really believe it was true, but it was better not to take any chances. They decided to take Gamaliel's advice.

They ordered the apostles to be beaten and warned them not to speak about Jesus anymore. But they set them free.

And every day, in the Temple and at home, the apostles preached and taught that Jesus was the Savior. They even thanked God that they had been allowed to suffer for Jesus!

33. Danger, Death, and a Growing Church

In the synagogue of the Freedmen, a young Jew named Stephen was telling the good news of Jesus. The believers in Jerusalem loved Stephen. They liked his friendly ways and his warm smile. They liked the way his eyes glowed and his voice grew strong and glad when he told what Jesus had done for them. Truly God was speaking through this man, they thought. The apostles had even chosen him to be one of their special helpers.

But most of the believers would not have understood what Stephen was saying now. He was speaking in Greek, the language of the Jews who worshiped in the synagogue of the Freedmen. Stephen himself was a Greek Jew. He wanted all the Greek Jews to believe in Jesus.

The men who were listening to Stephen understood perfectly well what he was saying. And many of them did not like it at all! How dare this man say that Jesus was the Christ! He was even saying that Jesus was greater than Moses!

Some of them had tried to argue with Stephen, but his answers were always so good that he made them feel foolish. The Greek Jews did not like to feel foolish. They did not like Stephen. They wanted to get rid of him.

So these Greek Jews who did not believe in Jesus spread false stories about Stephen.

"This man is trying to turn the Jews against Moses," they said. "We have even heard him say terrible things about God!"

Some people believed the lies about Stephen. "The rulers shall hear about this!" they said.

Before Stephen knew what was happening, angry men seized his arms. Angry voices sounded in his ears. He was being taken to the court of the high priest.

"What has this man done?" the high priest asked.

Then false witnesses said, "This man talks against our Temple and the Law of Moses. We have even heard him say that this Jesus will destroy the Temple and change the laws that Moses gave us."

The rulers looked at Stephen. How could he look so calm?

"Is this true?" the high priest asked him.

Then Stephen replied, "Brothers and fathers, listen to me. You all know how the holy God made his promises to Abraham. And Abraham became the father of Isaac, and Isaac became the father of Jacob, and Jacob became the father of twelve sons."

The rulers looked at one another. Surely there was nothing wrong with what the young Jew was saying.

Stephen went on. "You know, too, how Joseph's brothers were jealous and sold him as a slave. But God was with him, and Joseph became governor of Egypt and saved the land from famine. When Joseph's brothers came down to Egypt to buy grain, they found Joseph there. And he forgave them for what they had done to him, and he brought all his family to Egypt to live.

"And you know how after many years in Egypt, a new king made our fathers slaves. But God chose Moses to rescue his people. He led them out of Egypt with many wonders and signs. And when they came to Mount Sinai, God made a covenant with our fathers. He chose them to be his people, and he promised to be their God. He gave them his laws to guide them. But our fathers grumbled and would not obey Moses. They even asked Aaron to make a golden calf for them to worship instead of God."

The rulers of Israel nodded. It was all true. They could find nothing wrong with what Stephen said.

Stephen talked about Joshua, who had led the people into Canaan. He talked about the great King David, and about David's son Solomon, who built a temple for God.

But what was this? What was Stephen saying now? The rulers and the high priest leaned forward to listen.

"If you think that God lives in the Temple, you are wrong," Stephen said. "God does not live in houses that men

MEN OF PENTECOST

Danger, Death, and a Growing Church 269

make. How can the God who made the whole world fit in one small building? God is everywhere with his people! Jerusalem is not the only place where men can know and love and worship God."

Stephen saw that the rulers did not like what he was saying. His voice became stern.

"You stubborn people!" he said. "You never listen to God. You are just like your fathers, who hurt and killed God's prophets. God himself chose you to be his servants, but you killed his Son Jesus. You murdered the Savior!"

Now the rulers were so angry that they ground their teeth. But Stephen looked up toward the sky and exclaimed, "Look! I see Jesus standing at God's right hand."

The rulers of Israel put their hands over their ears so that they would not hear anything more. Many rushed forward and grabbed Stephen. They dragged him outside and threw stones at him until he died. But before he died, they heard him pray in a loud voice, "Lord, do not hold this sin against them."

And those who saw him on that day said that his face was like the face of an angel.

DANGER FOR THE CHURCH

In the crowd that day was another young Jew named Saul. He did not throw any stones at Stephen. He only took care of the coats of the other men. But Saul was glad to see Stephen die. He hated these followers of Jesus! He wished he could get rid of them all.

Saul and others like him soon made Jerusalem a dangerous place for the followers of Jesus to be. No believer was safe. Saul himself went from house to house, searching and questioning. He ordered many men and women to be dragged off to prison.

In those days of danger, the followers of Jesus often thought of Stephen. They knew that more of them would die in the same way if they kept on talking about Jesus. Many of them packed their belongings and left the city. Some went to other towns in Judea. Some went to Samaria. Still others went even farther north, trying to escape from Saul.

But they did not stop talking about Jesus. Everywhere they went, they told others about their Lord. They were his witnesses in all Judea and Samaria!

Instead of stopping the church, Saul and the unbelieving Jews were helping it to grow!

Part 10

A Mighty Witness

34. Saul in Damascus

"Saul is coming!"

"Saul is coming here!"

The fearful news spread quickly among the believers in the city of Damascus. It meant danger for the followers of Jesus even in this city far north of Jerusalem.

"Is it true?" the followers of Jesus asked their leader Ananias.

"It is true," Ananias told them. "Even now he may be in the city."

The followers were afraid. They remembered what had happened to their friends in Jerusalem. They knew what this would mean: Houses searched. Followers questioned and thrown into prison. Danger and death for the believers in Jesus.

"He has orders to find the followers in every synagogue," Ananias said quietly. "He has permission to bring every believer back to Jerusalem—in chains."

"We shall all be murdered!" some cried.

"Or taken to prison—"

"We thought we were safe here," others said.

"No one is safe from this terrible Saul. He has made a promise that he will get rid of all of us and he means to keep his promise. There is no hope for us now."

"There is always hope," Ananias reminded his friends. "We believe in a living Lord. He will not leave us. Why should we fear death? Even death cannot keep us from the Lord Jesus!"

"What shall we do?" someone asked.

"Go home," Ananias said. "Wait—and pray."

That night the Lord spoke to Ananias.

"Ananias," he called.

"I am here, Lord," Ananias answered.

Then the Lord said to him, "Get up and go to the street called 'Straight.' When you come to the house of Judas, ask for a man named Saul from Tarsus. He knows you are coming. I have told him that you will place your hands upon him so that he may see again."

Ananias was so surprised he could scarcely talk. "Lord," he gasped, "I have heard about this man Saul! I know what

he has done to harm your people in Jerusalem. I know that he has come here to arrest all who call on your name!"

But the Lord said to him, "Go. I have chosen this man to preach my name to Gentiles and kings, as well as to the Jews."

Ananias got up. How shaky his legs felt! It was a long walk to the street called "Straight." He stumbled through the darkness. There was no moon. The sky was empty of stars. Ananias heard his heart pounding like an echo to his footsteps.

He walked through the lonely night—and wondered. Saul of Tarsus! That this man who hated the followers of Jesus so fiercely would ever become a witness for Jesus—no, Ananias could not imagine that.

And what was this about helping Saul to see again? Ananias had never heard that Saul was blind. Strange that nobody had told him. Maybe it was not the same Saul, Ananias thought hopefully. But in his heart he knew that it was. The closer Ananias came to the house, the more he felt like running away. Still, the Lord had told him to go, and so Ananias obeyed.

Judas was waiting at the door. He took his friend's arm. "I was going to send for you," he said in a low voice, "but Saul told me he knew you were coming. I tell you, Ananias, I have never seen such a thing. The Lord is truly with us! This Saul—this terror whom we have all feared—he has been here in my house for three days. He has said almost nothing. He has not eaten or had anything to drink. And the man is blind—blinded by a light from heaven, he says. Come in. I will show you."

Ananias went inside. He stared at the helpless-looking man who sat with his head buried in his hands. Surely this was not the fierce enemy of the followers of Jesus. He stepped closer.

"Saul—brother," he said. "Saul, the Lord has sent me so that you may see again and so that you may be filled with the Holy Spirit."

Ananias put his hands on Saul's head. At once, something white and flaky like scales fell from the troubled man's eyes. He could see again!

That night Saul was baptized. And on the next day he went to the synagogue, telling everyone that Jesus was the Son of God. Those who had trembled in fear listened in amazement. They did not know what to think.

"Isn't this the same man who did such terrible things to the followers in Jerusalem?" they asked each other. "Isn't this the man who came to Damascus with orders to arrest us?"

Saul continued to surprise everyone with his preaching. He had seen the risen Lord! Now he would be a witness and a follower of Jesus.

35. Good News to the Gentiles

The church at Antioch in Syria to the leaders of the church in Jerusalem: Joy and peace from God the Father and from our Lord Jesus Christ!

Strange and wonderful things have happened to us in this strange city since we fled from Jerusalem. At first we witnessed to other Jews only. But there are not many in Antioch. And when believers from Cyprus and Cyrene came here, they spoke to the Greeks also. Many who are not Jews now believe in Jesus. They worship with us and share in all that we do. We have witnessed everywhere in his name, and the Lord has added many new followers to his family.

We have heard of no other place where the good news is being preached to Gentiles. Are we doing wrong? Still, we cannot help but believe that God has done this and that we are doing what he wants.

There are some here who laugh at us and call us a new name—Christians. They are making fun of us, but we are proud to be Christians—followers of the Lord Jesus Christ!

Perhaps a letter like this one brought news of what was happening at Antioch to Jerusalem. The leaders of the church were horrified. Gentiles in the church! Surely there must be some mistake. They had never had anything to do with people who were not Jews. How could God's message be for those who did not follow Jewish laws and customs?

Finally they sent Barnabas to Antioch to find out what was happening.

But when Barnabas saw that many Greeks really did believe in Jesus, he was glad. "Surely this is God's work," he said. "Now we know that God wants all people to be part of his family—not just the Jews."

A MIGHTY WITNESS

So Barnabas stayed in Antioch, preaching and teaching. From the nearby city of Tarsus he brought a friend to help him. It was Saul. How surprised the followers must have been to find their old enemy witnessing for Jesus!

For a whole year, Saul and Barnabas stayed with the Christians in Antioch, and day by day the church grew larger and stronger.

But a new adventure was waiting for Saul and Barnabas. God had another job for them to do. He wanted them to take the good news of Jesus to other lands, too. When the Christians at Antioch were sure that this was what God wanted, they blessed Saul and Barnabas and sent them away.

Good News to the Gentiles

"We shall miss you," they told the two men. "But we shall pray for you and your new work. Through you God will help many people to learn of Jesus."

No one in Antioch guessed that they were sending the new missionaries straight into trouble and danger. No one dreamed of the exciting things that were about to happen!

ANOTHER ANTIOCH

In the Roman province of Pisidia there was another city named Antioch. The rulers of the synagogue welcomed the two visitors. "Have you any message for the people?" they asked politely.

The shorter man stood up. He looked at the faces of the worshipers. Would they believe what he had to tell them, he wondered.

"Men of Israel, and all who fear God," he said, "my name is Paul, and this man beside me is Barnabas. We are from Antioch in Syria. We have come because God has given us the most important message in the world."

The Jews looked at one another in wonder. What could this mean? Who was this man who called himself Paul?

They listened as Paul reminded them of the promises God had made to their fathers. They liked the way he spoke of Abraham and Moses and the great King David.

"This is a wise man," they told each other.

"And now God has brought to Israel a Savior, Jesus, as he promised," Paul was saying. "Those who live in Jerusalem killed Jesus, but God raised him from the dead. His disciples are witnesses that he is alive again. Through this Jesus you are forgiven for all your sins!"

What great excitement there was in the synagogue at Antioch that day! The Jews begged Paul and Barnabas to come back the next Sabbath and talk to them again. Many of them followed the missionaries to hear more.

The next week it seemed that the whole city was gathered at the synagogue. The Jews were jealous that so many people had come.

"Why, some of them are not even Jews!" they said. They decided to make trouble for the apostles.

"Don't listen to these men!" they said. "They do not tell us the truth!"

Then Paul said, "You foolish men! The message we have is from God. We brought it to you first, because you are Jews. You have known the promises of God from the beginning. But if you will not listen, we will take our message to the Gentiles. For God has commanded us to bring his Word to all people!"

Many of the Gentiles listened and were glad. But the Jews told the important people of the town that Paul and Barnabas had come to make trouble. Antioch became a city of danger for the apostles. Finally they were forced to leave.

But they went on to the next town, and the next. And wherever they went the Holy Spirit gave them courage to tell the news that Jesus is the Savior.

36. Witnesses in Prison

Lydia walked slowly away from the busy marketplace of Philippi. On other days she had always stopped to talk with the merchants about the purple-dyed cloth she sold. She did not see the dancing shadows that followed a little group of children as they skipped along the edges of the street. She did not hear the young men singing on their way home from work. At first she did not even hear the friends who called her name.

"Lydia!" The two women ran toward their friend. "Lydia!" they called again. This time Lydia heard them.

"Do you know what has happened to Paul and Silas?" Estella asked.

"Is it true that they are in prison?" Rachel wanted to know.

Lydia nodded. It was true. "Paul healed a slave girl who told fortunes," she told her friends. "The girl's owners were angry because their business was ruined. So they told the city officials that Paul and Silas were trying to get people to follow ways that are against the Roman law."

Rachel began to cry. "What will happen to us without Paul and Silas to help us?" she wept.

Lydia put her arm around her friend's shoulder. "Don't cry, Rachel," she said. "God will show us a way to go on with his work. But now we must pray for Paul and Silas."

Lydia left her friends and started to walk toward home. She wondered what would happen next. Perhaps all the followers of Jesus would be in trouble now. She decided not to go directly home after all. Instead, she turned down another street and walked out beyond the city gate to the place of prayer at the riverside. This was the meeting place for the small group of Jews in Philippi. Here they had first listened to Paul preach.

Lydia sat on the bank of the narrow river. She remembered the day she had been baptized here. She looked across the plain to the next range of mountains and thought of a psalm she and her friends often sang:

"I lift up my eyes to the hills.
   From whence does my help come?
My help comes from the LORD,
   who made heaven and earth.
The LORD will keep you from all evil;
   he will keep your life.
The LORD will keep
   your going out and your coming in
   from this time forth and for evermore."

"Lord Jesus," Lydia prayed softly, "keep Paul and Silas this night. Help them to know that you are near. Give them courage, whatever happens. And help us to trust your power and care."

It was growing dark when at last Lydia went home. There she waited and wondered and prayed.

In their prison cell Paul and Silas were also praying and singing hymns. The other prisoners and the jailer listened in amazement. What kind of God did these men have? Their robes were torn; their bodies were stiff and sore from the beating they had been given; their feet were fastened in stocks. But they were singing songs of praise to God!

About midnight there was a terrible noise, like the rumble of thunder deep in the earth. The whole prison shook like a tree caught in the lash of a wild, wild storm. Lamps rolled to the floor and lost their flames in the damp, loose earth. Dishes were tossed into the air and crashed against the walls.

Suddenly the doors of the prison blew wide open with a great rush of wind. The prisoners threw up their arms in terror. Their chains came loose from the stone walls. They pushed their way through the darkness toward Paul and Silas.

"Hurry, we can escape," they cried. "We are free!"

But Paul reached out to them. "Stay where you are," he commanded. "And give God thanks for this night."

When the jailer saw the doors wide open, he was sure that all his prisoners had escaped. He drew his sword to kill himself before the officials could find out what had happened.

A MIGHTY WITNESS

But Paul called out to him, "Do not hurt yourself! We are all here!"

Quickly the jailer sent for new lights. He rushed into the inner prison. There he saw all his prisoners waiting. Trembling and frightened, he fell down at the feet of Paul and Silas.

"Now I know that your God is very great," he said. "Sirs, what must I do to be saved?"

Paul helped the man to his feet. "Believe in the Lord Jesus," he said, "and you will be saved—you and all your household."

The jailer took Paul and Silas to his house. He washed their wounds and gave them food. There, in the early morning hours, the missionaries told the jailer and his family all that God had done through Jesus. And they believed and were baptized.

When daylight came, the Roman officials heard about the night's strange happenings. They were afraid to keep Paul and Silas in prison, so they sent soldiers with orders to let the men go. But Paul surprised them. He refused to leave!

"We were beaten in public without any trial," he said, "and then we were thrown into prison. We are Roman citizens, and the officials had no right to treat us that way. If they are ready to let us go, let them come and take us out of prison themselves."

Roman citizens! When the officials heard this, they were more frightened than ever. What if the governor heard about this! Quickly they came and apologized to Paul and Silas.

They took them out of the prison and asked them to leave the city.

But Paul went first to Lydia's house. He wanted his friends to know that he and Silas were safe.

"I shall always thank God for you, my friends," Paul told them. "You must continue to grow in love and bring others to Christ. I will pray for your work. I will write to you along the way."

So Paul left to take the good news to other cities also. And the little church at Philippi grew strong and witnessed bravely in the name of Jesus.

37. Trouble in Jerusalem

From the Tower of Antonia the Roman tribune could look down into the Temple courtyard. What he saw worried him. It was a festival, and once more the Temple was crowded with visitors. But something was wrong, the tribune thought. The people below were angry about something. What was all that noise, he wondered. What were they shouting about?

"Go down and find out what is happening," he told one of his soldiers.

Minutes before, some Jews from Asia had seen Paul go into the Temple with a young man. All at once angry voices were shouting, "There he is! There is the man who has been teaching men everywhere to hate the Jews and our Law and this holy place. Look! He has even brought a Gentile into the Temple!"

No one stopped to see whether it was true. No one waited to hear what Paul had to say. No one looked to find out whether the young man really was a Gentile. If they had, they would have seen that he was a Jew. Paul was not breaking any law.

Yelling and screaming, the crowd rushed into the Temple and seized Paul. "Kill him!" they shouted as they dragged him outside.

When the soldier saw the mob beating Paul, he raced back to the tower. "They have gone crazy!" he gasped. "They are killing a man!" At once the tribune took soldiers and centurions and ran to the crowd.

The crowd quieted when they saw the Roman officer and his men. Paul, already badly beaten, was arrested and bound in chains.

"Who is this man?" the tribune asked. "What has he done?"

With a great noise the answers came. Some shouted one thing, some another. Nothing was clear. So the tribune ordered Paul taken to the barracks for questioning. The soldiers had to carry him because the crowd kept pushing and shoving and shouting, "Away with him! Kill him!"

When they got to the top of the steps, Paul said to the tribune in Greek, "Please let me have a chance to speak to these people."

The tribune was surprised that Paul spoke Greek. "Well, I suppose it will do no harm," he said.

Paul stood on the steps and raised his arms to show that he had something to say. When it was quiet, he began to speak in the Hebrew language, the language the people knew best.

"I am a Jew," Paul told them. "I was born in Tarsus, but I grew up right here in Jerusalem. Gamaliel was my teacher. Like you, I learned to fear God and keep his laws. For a long time I even had the followers of Jesus thrown into prison and put to death.

"But one day on the road to Damascus I was blinded by a great light. And the Lord Jesus himself spoke to me. Those who were with me guided me into Damascus, for I could not see. Then Ananias came to me and I could see again. And he said, 'The God of our fathers has chosen you to be a witness to all men that Jesus is the Christ, the living Lord.'

"So I was baptized, and God forgave all my sins. From that day, I have been a follower of Jesus and have preached his name. I even tried to preach here in Jerusalem, but no one here would believe me. So the Lord sent me far away to the Gentiles."

Now the Jews had heard enough. They could not believe that God wanted Gentiles to be part of his family.

"Kill him!" they screamed again. "Such a man is not fit to live!" They shouted and threw dust in the air.

"Take this man inside," the tribune ordered. "Beat him until he admits what he has done wrong."

So the soldiers tied Paul with leather thongs and were getting ready to beat him. But Paul said to a centurion, "Is it right for you to beat a Roman citizen who has had no trial at all?"

Then the centurion hurried to the tribune. "Do you know what you almost did?" he asked the tribune. "This man is a Roman citizen!"

"Is that true?" the tribune asked Paul.

"Yes," Paul answered. "My father was a Roman citizen and so am I."

Now the tribune was afraid. What should he do with Paul? One thing he knew: He must protect him from the Jews!

A PLOT THAT FAILED

A few days later a frightened youth came to the barracks to see Paul. He was Paul's nephew. What he had to say made Paul call one of the soldiers.

"Take him to the tribune at once," he said. "He has something very important to say."

When the tribune saw the youth, he took him by the hand and said to him, "Don't be afraid. What do you have to tell me?"

"It's—it's the Jews!" the youth stammered. "They want to kill Paul! They have made a plot to get him out of the barracks. They are going to pretend that they only want to ask questions. But more than forty men lie in ambush. They have sworn not to eat or drink anything until they have killed my uncle Paul!"

Trouble in Jerusalem   293

The tribune's face was serious. "All right, lad," he said. "They won't get away with it. Now go. And do not tell anyone that you have told me this."

That night, as soon as it was dark, two hundred soldiers, with seventy horsemen and two hundred bodyguards, took Paul secretly to Caesarea. There Paul waited for the Roman governor—and a new adventure.

A MIGHTY WITNESS

38. Shipwreck—and a New Chance

What should be done with the prisoner Paul? The Roman governor, Felix, did not know. He listened to the Jews, who came and called Paul a troublemaker and a ringleader of the Christians. But what had he done? He had not been stirring up a crowd. He had only been bringing offerings to the Temple. It was true that he was a Christian; he said so himself. But he still obeyed Jewish law, and he worshiped the same God the Jews worshiped.

"I will decide later," Felix said. But two years later, when a new governor came to take his place, he still could not make up his mind. So he left Paul in prison to please the Jews.

What should be done with the prisoner Paul? The new governor, Festus, did not know the answer either. It did not seem to him that Paul had done anything very wrong. But he knew that the Jews wanted to kill Paul, and Festus wanted to please the Jews.

Finally Paul himself answered the question. "I have done no harm to the Jews," he told Festus. "I will not let you turn me over to them. I am a Roman citizen. I want to go to Rome. Caesar himself shall hear my story."

STORMY WEATHER

Everything was ready. The sailors had finished loading the ship. The great sail was ready for hoisting. Paul and his friend Luke, who was going with him, said good-bye to their friends. They boarded the ship with the Roman centurion, Julius, and set sail for Rome.

Winter was coming. Fierce north winds had started to sweep across the sea. Could the ship make it before the winter storms began? At Myra, Paul and the other prisoners were taken aboard another ship bound for Rome. In the high wind at sea the old ship creaked and groaned. Julius became more and more worried.

"Already we have lost many days," he told Paul. "If this wind gets worse, we won't be able to go on at all."

At a harbor called Fair Haven, on the island of Crete, the ship found shelter. By this time the winds were so strong that it seemed too dangerous to go any further.

"We are headed for trouble," Paul warned Julius and the captain. "If we go on, we will surely lose the ship and the cargo, and maybe even our lives."

"But we can't stay in this harbor all winter," the captain said.

When the wind suddenly changed to a mild breeze, the captain thought he could sail the ship to a safer harbor. But before long a tremendous gale swept down, driving the ship off its course. The ship bucked and tossed; high waves splashed over the deck. The second day the crew began to throw the cargo overboard to lighten the ship. Then the tackle went. Soon the food supplies would have to go, too.

For days the storm covered the sea with darkness. No sun shone by day; no stars lighted the way by night. Splinters of wood from the swaying mast flew through the air, and the salt spray burned the faces of the men. The sailors gave up hope of being saved.

"Be brave," Paul told the men. "God wants me to witness in Rome. I believe that God will save me and all the men on this ship."

On the fourteenth night of the storm the wind dropped. The sailors tested the depth of the water.

"Twenty fathoms!" came the call. Land must be nearby!

The order was given to test again. This time the cry came back, "Fifteen fathoms!"

"Throw out the anchors!" commanded the captain.

Four anchors were thrown from the stern of the ship. Through the long night the men waited for dawn. When daylight finally came, they could see a sandy beach in the distance. The men cut away the anchors that held the ship and ran up the foresail. The wind slipped into the little sail and drove the ship toward shore.

Suddenly the ship's bottom scraped against hidden rocks. The bow stuck fast. The stern was smashed to pieces by the pounding waves.

"Hurry!" shouted Julius. "All those who can swim—jump! The rest of you, hold on to anything that floats! Don't wait —jump!"

The ship was completely wrecked. But everyone on board came safely to the island of Malta, and there they spent the winter.

A MIGHTY WITNESS

When spring came, a new ship took them on to Rome. And Paul had his chance to witness in the capital city of the empire.

Luke laid down his pen. His story was finished. Witnesses for Jesus had told the good news in Jerusalem and in all Judea and Samaria. They had carried it all the way to the mighty city of Rome. They would keep on spreading the news, even to the end of the earth.

Shipwreck—and a New Chance

ALTAR. A raised place, often a mound of stones, used for sacrifice and burning incense.

AMOS. A shepherd prophet who spoke for God in the Northern Kingdom.

ANANIAS (an-uh-*nigh*-uhs). A Christian leader who lived in Damascus.

ANATHOTH (*an*-uh-thoth). The village near Jerusalem where Jeremiah was born.

ANOINT. To apply a special oil as a sign that someone or something was set apart for God's service.

ANTIOCH (*an*-tee-ahk). An important city in Syria where a large number of Jews lived. Here Jesus' followers were first called *Christians*.

APOSTLE. The first Christian leaders who were sent to preach and teach. The twelve disciples were apostles, as were Paul and Barnabas.

ARAMAIC (air-reh-*may*-ik). The language which Jesus and his disciples spoke.

ARK OF THE COVENANT. A sacred chest which was a sign of God's presence.

ASSYRIA. The homeland of fierce soldiers who destroyed the Northern Kingdom.

ATHENS. A large and important city in Greece.

BABYLON (*bab*-uh-lon). The beautiful city that served as capital of Babylonia.

BABYLONIA (bab-uh-*low*-nee-uh). Land of the people who destroyed Jerusalem and took the people of the Southern Kingdom into exile.

BARNABAS (*bar*-nuh-bus). One of the first Christian missionaries. He and Paul worked together.

BEROEA (beh-*ree*-ah). A town in Macedonia where Paul preached.

BETHLEHEM. A town in Judea about five miles south of Jerusalem. The home of the family of David.

BETHSAIDA (beth-*say*-ih-duh). A fishing village on the northern shore of the Sea of Galilee, near Capernaum.

BETRAY. To be a traitor; to turn over to an enemy someone who trusts and needs you.

BLASPHEMER (blas-*feem*-er). Someone who says terrible things about God; someone who lies by claiming to be like God.

CAESAR (*see*-zer). A title given to the ruler of the Roman Empire.

CAESAREA (*sess*-uh-*ree*-uh). A city on the coast of Palestine.

Words, Names, and Places

CAESAREA PHILIPPI (*sess*-uh-*ree*-uh *fil*-uh-pie). A Roman city in northern Palestine. Also the countryside around the city.

CANAAN (*kay*-nan). The land between the Jordan River and the Mediterranean Sea. The land promised to the Hebrews.

CAPERNAUM (kuh-*per*-nay-um). A town on the Sea of Galilee where Jesus often stopped.

CAVE OF ADULLAM. A secret cave near the city of Adullam that served as David's headquarters.

CENTURION (sen-*tur*-ee-uhn). A Roman soldier who commanded a hundred men.

CHRIST. A Greek word for Messiah. It means "the Anointed One," or the Savior sent by God.

CORINTH. One of the most important cities in Greece.

COVENANT. A solemn agreement. God's promise to the Hebrews to be their God and the Hebrews' promise to be his people.

CYPRUS (*sigh*-pruss). An island in the Mediterranean Sea. Barnabas was born here.

CYRENE (sigh-*ree*-nee). A large city in northern Africa where many Jews lived.

DAMASCUS (duh-*mass*-kus). The most important city in Syria.

DERBE (*durr*-bee). A town in Asia Minor which Paul visited.

DESCENDANTS. All the people who are descended from a particular person—his children and his children's children's children.

DESPAIR. A terrible feeling of being all alone and without hope.

DISCIPLE. A word that means "learner" or "pupil." Jesus had many disciples; the Twelve were men who had been specially chosen.

ELDERS. A group of leaders who acted as a court for the Jews.

ELIJAH (ih-*lie*-juh). An Old Testament prophet who spoke for God in the Northern Kingdom. In Jesus' time people thought Elijah would come again to announce the Messiah.

EMMAUS (ee-*may*-us). A village near Jerusalem.

EPHESUS (*eff*-uh-sus). A large Roman seaport city in Asia Minor.

EXILE. Forcing a person to leave his own country. The time when the Jews were captured and taken to faraway Babylonia.

EZEKIEL (ih-*zee*-kyuhl). A prophet who spoke for God during the long exile in Babylonia.

FAMINE (*fam*-uhn). A time when food is scarce and people are hungry.

Words, Names, and Places

FELIX (*fee*-liks). The Roman governor of Judea who kept Paul in prison for two years.

FESTUS (*fes*-tuhs). The Roman ruler who sent Paul to Rome.

GALATIA (guh-*lay*-shah). A region Paul visited in central Asia Minor.

GALILEE. The rich, fruitful land in northern Palestine where Jesus grew up.

GAMALIEL (guh-*may*-lih-el). A famous teacher of the Law. Paul was one of his students.

GETHSEMANE (geth-*sem*-uh-nee). An olive grove near Jerusalem. Jesus prayed in this garden the night he was arrested.

GOLGOTHA (*gahl*-guh-thuh). The name of the hill near Jerusalem where Jesus was crucified.

HARAN (*hair*-un). An old and important trading city. Abraham left Haran to go to Canaan.

HEBREWS. A name the Bible gives to Abraham and his descendants.

HOSEA (ho-*zay*-uh). A prophet in the Northern Kingdom who spoke of God's love.

HYSSOP (*hiss*-up). A small, bushy plant with a spicy smell.

ICONIUM (eye-*koh*-nih-um). A city Paul and Barnabas visited on their first missionary journey.

IDOL. A statue or any other object that is worshiped.

ISRAEL. The new name God gave Jacob. Jacob's twelve sons and their tribes and all their descendants are called "children of Israel" or Israelites. The Northern Kingdom was also called Israel.

JERICHO (*jer*-ih-ko). A warm, pleasant city in Judea, near the northern end of the Dead Sea.

JERUSALEM. The most important city in Palestine.

JEWS. The name given to people from Judah as they returned from exile. Later used to mean all Hebrews, or children of Israel.

JOSHUA (*josh*-oo-uh). The man who led the Hebrews into Canaan after Moses died.

JOSIAH (jo-*sigh*-uh). A king of Judah who tried to bring his people back to God's ways.

JUDEA (jew-*dee*-uh). The hilly southern part of Palestine.

LEBANON. The mountainous land north of Israel; famous for its forests of cedar trees.

LYSTRA (*liss*-truh). One of the small towns Paul and Barnabas visited.

MANNA. Tiny sweet-tasting flakes or seeds which the Hebrews found on the ground every morning during their wilderness journey.

Words, Names, and Places

MESSIAH. A Hebrew word that means "the Anointed One." The Jewish people were waiting for the Messiah, or Savior, whom God would send.

MYRRH (*murr*). A sweet-smelling gum found on desert bushes. Used as perfume and medicine and for anointing.

NAIN. A small village in Galilee, near Nazareth.

NAZARETH. The small town in Galilee where Jesus grew up.

PALESTINE. An old name for the land of the Hebrews. It is still used today.

PARABLE. A short story that shows an important truth.

PERGA (*purr*-gah). A city Paul and Barnabas visited in Asia Minor.

PERSECUTE. To hurt a person because of what he believes.

PHARAOH (*fair*-oh). A title given to the kings of Egypt.

PHARISEES (*fair*-uh-seez). A group of important Jews who believed that God wanted their people to obey every exact detail of the Jewish laws.

PHILIPPI (*fil*-uh-pie). The first town in Europe in which Paul preached.

PHILISTINES (*fil*-uh-stines). A warlike people who lived along the seacoast in southern Palestine.

PISIDIA (pie-*sid*-ih-ah). A mountainous region which Paul visited in Asia Minor.

POTIPHAR (*pot*-ih-fer). The Egyptian officer who bought Joseph to be his slave.

REHOBOAM (ree-uh-*bow*-um). King Solomon's son. The first king of the Southern Kingdom.

RIGHTEOUS. Good or holy. A person who does what God wants.

SABBATH. A Hebrew word that means "cease." The Bible says that one day each week should be for God; a day when work "ceases" or stops.

SACRIFICE. A gift offered to God. Old Testament laws said that only the best living animals or fruits or vegetables could be used.

SADDUCEES (*sad*-you-sees). A group of rich Jewish families who took care of the Temple and tried to preserve ancient Jewish ways.

SAMARIA. The capital city of the Northern Kingdom. Also the hilly, central part of Palestine.

SCRIBES. Lawyers, experts in the Law of Moses. They taught the Jewish people about their laws.

SCRIPTURE. A word that means "writing"; the Bible. For people in Jesus' day, the Old Testament.

SYNAGOGUE (*sin*-ih-gahg). A place of worship. After the Temple in Jerusalem was destroyed, the Jews built synagogues in almost every village.

SYRIA (*seer*-ih-uh). An old kingdom to the northeast of Palestine. In Jesus' time, a small area ruled by the Romans.

TABERNACLE. A tent in which the Hebrews kept the Ark during their desert wanderings.

TARSUS. The city in Asia Minor where Paul was born.

TEKOA (tih-*ko*-uh). A town in the hills of Judah, the home of Amos the prophet.

THEOPHILUS (thee-*ahf*-ih-lus). A name that means "friend of God." The person for whom Luke wrote the Gospel of Luke and the Book of Acts.

THESSALONICA (*thess*-uh-low-*nigh*-kah). An important trading city where there were many Christians.

TOWER OF ANTONIA (an-*toe*-nih-ah). A tower at the northwestern end of the Temple court. Roman soldiers lived there and kept watch over the courtyard.

TRIBE. A group of families who live together as one large family; a clan.

TROAS (*tro*-ass). A seaport city Paul visited briefly several times.

WILDERNESS. A word Bible writers used to mean a desert or dry, sandy, rocky country.

ZEALOTS (*zell*-uhts). Jews who thought the Messiah would be a great army leader. Many were outlaws who lived in the hills and looked for ways to harm the Romans.

ZEDEKIAH (zed-uh-*ki*-uh). The last king of Judah. He did not listen to Jeremiah the prophet.

ACKNOWLEDGMENT

Scripture quotations are from the *Revised Standard Version of the Bible,* copyrighted 1946 and 1952 by the Division of Christian Education, National Council of Churches, and are used by permission.